Kalli

A Spaniel's Life

Kalli

A Spaniel's Life

By
Laura Abbott

Arcola Creek
Press

Kalli: A Spaniel's Life

Published by
Arcola Creek Press

First American Paperback Edition

www.ArcolaCreekPress.com

Library Of Congress Control Number 2016906573

ISBN 978-0-9974161-0-7

Published in the United States of America

DEDICATION

For Marc, Kalli, and Petey.

Who else would be insane enough to join me on this journey?

And for the Kalli Fan Club.

You know who you are.

ACKNOWLEDGMENTS

My gratitude to my husband, Marc, knows no bounds. Your love and support throughout this project meant the world to me. And your lovely cover design, formatting, and tech support brought the book to life.

This book never would have seen the light of day if it hadn't been for Kalli. Her constant "encouragement" to get this project published provided the impetus to make it so. Thank you, Kalli...I think.

Kudos to my brilliant illustrator, Rian Miller. I don't know how you were able to capture Kalli's spirit so perfectly in your sketches, but I'm very grateful you did.

Many thanks to David Sutton. Your amazing photographs of Kalli have forever preserved her style and *joie de vivre* in a most tangible way.

Editors Elizabeth Delisi, Ray Rhamey, and Trace Edward Zaber helped whip this book into shape. I deeply appreciate your help.

And special thanks to Mary Monsell, Anne Pettis, and Dr. Kris Ahlberg. You supported this project every step of the way.

AUTHOR'S NOTE

This book is based on actual events. Names of people, dogs, and organizations have been changed.

CONTENTS

THE GIFT

I watched as a scowling elderly man hunched over a long line of shopping carts and pushed them across a parking lot broiling in the August sun. Squinting, he stared at the row of handles, his expression weary. He reached ahead with one hand to keep the carts under control.

With a wavery sigh, he stowed them by the overhang of the mega-grocery store and turned. Standing before him was a little black-and-white dog, her stub tail wiggling her entire butt. As his gaze reached her, Kalli promptly sat and smiled up at him.

He started to walk around her. She stood and blocked his path.

Catching his breath, he stopped, considering her.

Kalli's butt wiggled harder, a blur of English cocker spaniel energy. Timeless wisdom spilled out of brown eyes she drilled into him.

Hey! You're crying out for me right now. Even if you don't know it. So, pay attention. This is important, what I'm doing for you.

As if he'd heard her silent directive, he smiled slightly. Then the expression flickered and dimmed. "Kinda cute," he said in a dry, rusty voice.

Kalli responded by sitting on his feet. Her smile widened, and her eyebrows shot upward.

Light wreathed his face when he returned her grin. "You are definitely cute." He leaned down and tweaked her behind her floppy, graying black ears.

She licked his arm, and he chuckled. For a long moment, they studied each other.

What passed between them, I'll never know. It was a confidential exchange. But I had an idea. I'd seen the act before. I was observing a certified therapy dog interacting with a human in need. Kalli may have logged many hours in rehab centers throughout Chicago, but she didn't require a clinical setting to go to work. She was always on duty.

The power of Kalli, her ability to infuse humans with her joyous energy, never failed to thrill me. I'd learned years before to honor her finely honed instincts and let her have her head in a situation like this one. And so it was that I let the ice cream melt in my shopping bag without a trace of concern as I watched the pair.

The man stroked Kalli's back with slow, meditative motions. I could see the tension loosen in his body.

Finally, he straightened. Formerly dull eyes sparkled as he nodded to me. "Great dog." He entered the grocery store with a slight spring in his step, a faint whistle drifting from his lips.

He had accepted Kalli's gift.

JIGGER

It took my husband, Marc, and me years to fully appreciate Kalli's gifts. The road we traveled to reach that point was a joy...and a challenge. The journey began the day we picked up Angel—her puppy call name—from her breeder's house. So did the challenges.

It was a stifling July day. Marc was his usual unruffled self as we drove away from our home in Evanston, a North Shore suburb of Chicago, and began the trek to Michigan. I was nervous and excited. We were bringing home our baby. Life didn't get much more momentous for me. I was buzzing with so much adrenalin and anxiety, I practically vibrated. Barely containing myself, I settled into the seat and drew deep breaths, trying to be calm. And was actually succeeding—sort of—when we heard the sound of metal clanging under the car, then grating on pavement. The engine joined the cacophony as it screeched and wailed.

We'd lost our muffler in the middle of the Dan Ryan Expressway.

I looked out the side mirror in time to see the rusted hunk of metal bouncing across the lanes, finally coming to rest on the shoulder. I glared at the car part as it disappeared from my view, certain its death was a personal betrayal.

"What are we going to do?" I hollered at Marc over the screams of our car engine.

"What do you mean?"

"What do you mean, what do I mean? We can't drive to Pam's like this!"

"Why? Because of the muffler?"

I stared at Marc's unflappable profile, not believing what I was seeing and hearing. He wasn't in the least distressed by the disaster that had just struck.

He shrugged. "No harm, no foul. It landed well off the road, so it won't be a hazard to other drivers. No reason not to keep going. The car will drive fine without it. We're just going to be a little noisy."

"But, what will Pam think? I'll tell you what she'll think." (No need to waste a breath for him to answer when I already knew the correct response.) "She'll think we're pathetic people who can't take care of a car, much less one of her dogs." I drew a shaky breath. "She'll never let us adopt Angel now. Never. All the preparations, all the research and planning and—"

"Uh, Laura?"

"What?"

"Chill."

"I beg your pardon?" He was really annoying me with his calm, cool, and collected act. Except I knew it was no act. It was the real thing.

"You heard me. Honey, stuff happens. Mufflers fall off. It doesn't mean we're evil people who will starve our puppy and chain it to the radiator for the rest of its life."

"We don't have radiators." I stopped short and glanced over at Marc. He was valiantly smothering the hint of a smile. "If you start laughing at me, I swear I'll hit you—"

Whereupon Marc's laughter escaped. Right on cue. In between guffaws, he sputtered, "So…you're going to…hit me…with what? A muffler?"

In a flash, I saw a muffler sitting atop Marc's head. A giggle bubbled up from deep inside me. And I was furious at it. This was no time for humor. And yet…

Marc and I laughed all the way to Michigan.

And so it was that we bounced down the curving gravel driveway to Pam's single-story ranch house a few hours later with a growling motor and stifled chuckles on our lips. Vaguely, I was aware that something astonishing had happened. I'd been so busy giggling, I'd forgotten to be anxious.

Unfortunately, the reprieve didn't last long. As soon as my feet hit the ground, my nerves returned. And really, there was a lot for me to be nervous about.

Pam had been a bit…daunting…in her dealings with us once she knew we wanted to adopt one of her puppies. Neither Marc nor I ever had a job interview that rivaled the grilling we'd endured from the woman. We'd filled out long questionnaires demanding to know everything from how long we'd been married, to our employment history, to the size of our fenced-in yard. (The fact that we *had* a fenced-in yard was a given.) Character references had been mandatory, and a letter from the vet we used throughout the seventeen years of the life of our cat—now deceased—was a necessity. Our commitment to training the puppy was insisted upon.

Now, we faced this woman, who strode out of her house like a tank commander during the Battle of Prokhorovka (it was a famous tank engagement during World War Two, trust me). I barely stopped myself from jumping back into our deafening car and racing away.

She nodded to her right and spoke her first words to us. "Dogs are in the backyard."

So much for foreplay.

"Pam? Um, I'm Laura and this is—"

I'd started to extend my hand, but she had already turned her back on us, leading the way to the yard. Marc and I exchanged a quick look. I felt like I'd been caught with chewing gum in third grade and was being marched off to the principal's office.

"I won't lie to you"—Pam tossed her brisk words over her shoulder in our general direction—"these dogs are a handful. And Angel is a typical English cocker to the bone. She's full of herself. Should have seen her at the puppy show last week. Really something."

I froze, my fingers gripping the brand new leather leash I'd spent way too much time selecting. "Really something?" *What did that mean?*

Pam nodded. "She took over the ring. Loved the crowd immediately, and once she realized she could grab their attention by mimicking the show prance of my older dogs, she really went to town. Almost brought the house down with her perfect imitation of a Westminster performance. Quite the spectacle."

We passed through a gateway. Then, as Pam latched the gate behind us, I turned to face a sea of dogs. The backyard teemed with them—scrambling, careening English cocker spaniels as far as the eye could see. Most were black and white, officially known in spanieldom as blue roan. A few renegade reds and liver-and-tans gamboled across the grass as well. Long ears flapped and doggie grins spread wide as the animals bounced off and over each other like they were in a giant pinball machine. Waves of vibrant energy, bristling health, and mischievous humor hammered against me.

Panic struck. For months, I'd dreamt about taking home this dog. And now? All I wanted to do was run. And not *with* the pack. *Away* from it.

I started yelling at myself—in my head, not out loud. I might be neurotic, but I'm not crazy. *All right, Laura. Enough of this anxiety stuff. Yeah, this is a big deal. You're bringing home a baby* (my only baby since Marc and I had elected not to have human children). *But get a grip.*

You've prepared for this moment. Relax and enjoy. Or at the very least, center yourself, knock off the nerves, and try to be calm.

Actually, to say I "prepared" for the moment is a bit of an understatement. I live, eat, and breathe research on a regular day. That's an occupational hazard when one earns a living writing. When the research topic is important to me... Well, I'll let you extrapolate.

I'd launched Project Dog earlier that summer. It hadn't taken long for it to consume me. First burning issue? What type of dog to buy.

Finding the right breed is crucial for *anyone* adopting a canine pet, not just for those of us who tend toward the compulsive/obsessive end of the spectrum. And it's often overlooked by folks. The fact is, each breed has developed over time to be really good at something. The trick is to identify that something and figure out whether it fits your lifestyle.

I'd heard horror stories of high-energy Border collies literally going crazy when confined to a tiny run with no exercise or mental stimulation. Why? Because Border collies are workers to the bone. Their *raison d'être* is to apply their brilliant minds and agile bodies to the job at hand, such as herding. Not that you have to own sheep to adopt this animal. But their talents and tendencies need to be honored and exploited, whether it's on the agility course or in a field playing a high-powered game of Frisbee.

At the other end of the spectrum are those breeds placed on the Earth to provide human companionship, like the Shih Tzu. And then there are the pugs. They want to keep your lap warm, and eat any and all food they can find. Period. While a brisk walk is sometimes appreciated, these cunning little devils can thrive without tons of exercise if they have an involved owner to tease and manipulate.

Marc and I had taken careful stock of what we wanted in a dog and, in turn, what we could offer it. We were willing to exercise the beast every day, but not to the extent required by animals such as the high-energy Irish setter. (I'd had experience with those, having grown up with two red beauties. My family hadn't fulfilled the exercise requirement, and the animals had been hyper crazies.)

At this point in our lives, I was working from home while Marc travelled extensively for his job. So, our companion needed to be one I felt comfortable with and could handle alone. I didn't require a Schutzhund expert to protect me. Nor did I want to live with a couch potato. But our dog would have to be happy in a modest Dutch colonial with a small yard. Walks through the neighborhood and forays into the many parks within a few miles from our house were planned. Could our dog live with that?

Even though I knew they wouldn't fit into our lifestyle, the Irish setters of my youth kept trotting into my mind. Then one day, as I paged through yet another breed book—I had a stack of them teetering next to my desk—I discovered the sporting group. More specifically, the spaniels.

"They look like little setters!" I told Marc that evening. "They're perfect for us!"

He rolled his eyes. "Uh huh."

"Seriously, Marc. They are. I just know it."

He gave me a long look. "And if I had a dollar for every time you've found the perfect type of dog…"

"I know, you'd be wealthy. But this time I mean it."

In a measured tone, Marc said, "Well, that's great, Laura. I'm glad you've made a decision."

Bless his patience and his restraint. He could have pulled out the breed book that had zillions of dog-eared pages (no bad pun intended) indicating each "perfect for us" dog I'd identified over the weeks. But he didn't need to prove his point. We both know how I am.

Except, in this instance, I *really had* found the perfect type of dog. Rather than spend any more time trying to convince him, I joined an online spaniel discussion group and transferred my hyper research energy to them. Soon, I was peppering breeders and owners with questions. I stopped just short of being obnoxious and taking over the group—I think—and learned tons of stuff in the process.

The online experts told me the spaniel made a great family pet and was bred to be a flusher/retriever in the field. This meant it was intelligent with superior reasoning abilities and could work independently from its human, while still considered biddable— trained easily and was inclined to listen to its owners. Health issues varied among the types, though. And the severity seemed to be related to how well-known the animal was. For example, the American cocker and English springer spaniel tended to develop physical and behavioral problems because they were popular. Strong demand meant fertile ground for unscrupulous breeders to sell puppies at high volume without carefully monitoring genetics.

One type of spaniel intrigued me. Smaller in stature than most of its relatives, it seemed to be unknown among the general public and thus had been spared serious health complications. It was characterized as a "merry dog," and the big brown eyes and noble brow of the English cocker spaniel on the book page called to me.

I'd found my dog. Next step was to learn how to take care of it. Back to the online discussion groups to learn about all things ECS.

Let me just say it wasn't my intention to start an ugly war of words in the group. Really. But I hadn't been around dog people before, and I had no idea how *intense* they could get about things like rawhide chews (a choking menace or a distraction from heaven?) and prong collars (torture or training savior?). I learned more about lip folds and top lines than I ever wanted to know. And don't get them started about the exact perfect crate for an English cocker.

In the midst of the hysteria, a quiet voice reached out to me privately. It was a local breeder who had earned the respect of everyone in the group. She had a blue roan puppy available. Marc and I were in business.

So, you thought my research was crazy before? Now that an actual living and breathing animal was part of the mix, I went off on tangents that seemed nuts even to me. But, at the end of the process, my spare bedroom brimmed with a flawless collection of everything an ECS needed for an ideal life.

In center stage was a crate exquisitely proportioned to an English cocker body (the group had actually agreed about that item). Color-coordinated bumpers and fleece pads decorated its interior. They represented my demand for functional perfection, along with a high degree of cuteness and comfort.

Several food-and-water dish sets occupied one corner of the room. Their selection had taken days. Who knew there were so many choices? And how could I possibly limit myself to just a few?

Matching leashes and collars draped over the crate. I'd drowned in the cuteness thing where they were concerned and had spent an embarrassing amount of time agonizing over which color would perfectly accent the black-and-white fur of our puppy. I settled on bright red, making certain to buy collars that expanded as our baby grew.

Chew toys and stuffed animals, evaluated for days, were finally selected based upon the quality of their educational, calming, and entertainment values. Oh, and of course, their cuteness and safety. I ended up with a huge bin of them, most of which would be ignored in the years ahead.

And the books. Ah, the books. Ever-growing mountains of dog books sprung up in my already-cramped office, then spread to the rest of the house.

Piles of notes materialized on every available table top. I even lined up a trainer.

Now, as we stood in Pam's spacious, fenced-in yard, Marc chuckled and leaned down to whisper in my ear, "Any idea which puppy is ours?"

I shook my head. I'd been wondering the same thing ever since I saw the canine herd ranging behind the house.

In spite of myself, I felt my love for dogs take over my nerves. Leaning down, I cuddled a spaniel face in my hands after one of the lunatics decided to take time out from the race and sprawl across my boots.

A pink tongue raked across my fingers and a goofy grin spread across its face. It seemed to say:

You look like you could use some moral support.

Big brown orbs filled with canine love sparkled up at me. I just knew this dog had eyes for me and only me. Sorry, Marc.

"There's Angel's aunt." I followed Pam's pointing finger toward a particularly crazed black-and-white face framed by floppy ears. Tongue lolling, she pounced on a tennis ball and scooped it into her mouth. Two smaller English cockers rammed her from behind, and she tumbled across the muddy grass. The pair rolled over her in their quest for the ball. "And those two are cousins," Pam added.

"Who's this one?" I looked down at the dog still at my feet and scratched the liver-and-tan under its chin. I was in love, totally and completely. Could this sweetheart be my dog?

"That's Jigger."

Disappointment swirled through my gut and then guilt. Man, I hadn't even claimed my puppy yet, and I was already being unfaithful to her. "Any relation to Angel?"

"She's another cousin."

I looked into the deep brown of those eyes and fancied she had winked at me, as if this were all a big joke. I could have sworn she was saying:

You need to relax. This is supposed to be fun.

"And our dog? Which one—?"

"Oh, she's not out here, honey." Pam chuckled. "Just got her all cleaned up for you. I wasn't going to put her in this tomfoolery."

Feeling faintly relieved that even the breeder found the scrambling pack of dogs nutty, I followed the heavyset woman as she strode across the yard back toward the house. Marc stepped by my side, and Jigger trotted between us. We crossed an enclosed wraparound porch. Off to my right, a mountain of bird cages occupied one corner. Gem-colored parakeets twittered at us from within the metal enclosures. Evidently Pam's breeding talents were not limited to canines.

She opened a screen door and paused inside a tidy kitchen. Over her shoulder, I caught a glimpse of golden chintz, sparkling stainless steel appliances, and white cupboards. A terra cotta tile floor stretched before us, dotted with puppies.

"These are Angel's litter mates. At least, those still waiting to go to their new homes." Pam nodded toward them.

When she had first started to speak, they'd been fast asleep. But by the time she'd uttered her second word, brown eyes had popped open and wiggling bodies lurched onto sturdy legs.

So much for naptime.

Stubby tails—in this country, English cocker tails are docked right after birth—wagged in a blur as the babies raced toward us. Jigger maintained her post between Marc and me, eyeing the pandemonium with calm detachment, then pinning us with a purposeful look. I saw her message reflected in her eyes:

These ill-mannered young things can be so annoying.

The puppies ignored her as they attempted to scale our pants.

I leaned down to disentangle claws, my eyes scanning the room. Where was my dog?

And then I saw her. Wrapped in a towel, fresh from her bath, she curled around a stuffed bear on top of a pillow by a potbellied stove. Immune to the manic activity ranging around her, she was sound asleep.

Pam motioned us to a round oak table in one corner of the kitchen. "Let's get the paperwork out of the way while your dog catches up on her beauty sleep."

Still hopelessly attached to Jigger, I grabbed the nearest chair and began stroking her silky back while Marc sat next to Pam and across from me. Rifling through papers, the pair didn't notice an adult cocker, who strolled into the kitchen from an adjacent room. The animal took in the scene with a nonchalant glance, then hopped onto a chair by Marc. From there, she surveyed us with an arrogance I would have found amusing if I hadn't been so distracted.

Marc exchanged a quick glance with me. Dogs allowed to sit at the kitchen table?

As if Pam had heard his thoughts, she said, "Don't mind Rose. She's used to being at the table with us. Just ignore her if she bothers you."

Marc gave her a quick pat on the head, then turned back to the stack of paper in front of him. As Pam murmured, "That's Angel's mother, by the way," the dog nudged his arm with her muzzle.

Her intentions were so clear to me, it was as if I heard her speaking silently to Marc.

Hey, I'm an important part of this process. Pay attention to me.

He gave her a passing smile and continued signing his name on the dotted line. She bumped his arm, then drove her muzzle up through the gap formed by his crooked elbow.

He laughed and turned to her.

Evidently satisfied she'd received an appropriate amount of Marc's admiration, she yawned, jumped down, and started to walk from the room. At the doorway, she turned and fixed me with a stare. My head buzzed with her intent.

You're taking one of my babies. Be good to her, or you will be hearing from us.

I gripped the fur around Jigger's neck more tightly, and she looked up at me with her now-familiar smile.

Not to worry. You'll do just fine with her baby.

I studied Jigger for a long moment. Suddenly, a warming sensation swept over me. I'd never felt anything like it. It centered on the realization that this lovely creature had very purposefully gifted me with her steadiness and quiet affection in order to calm me.

And it had worked. Wow. Just…wow.

Meanwhile, as I was having this epiphany that changed my attitude toward dogs for the rest of my life, the mundane signing of paperwork ended. Pam scooped up the sleepy Angel with the words, "Let's get her groomed."

Jigger stayed close while we spent the next thirty minutes learning the ins and outs of English cocker fur styling. I listened for the first five minutes and then zoned out. There was no way in hell… Let me repeat that. No way *in hell* I would ever groom that dog. The mere sight of the stripping comb was enough to convince me of that.

Now, I know many folks groom their English cockers and love every minute of it. Bless their hearts. It's just that I'm not one of them. Hell, I barely get my own self to a hair stylist regularly. Usually, I slink into the shop with hair nearing my waist when the style is designed to sweep my shoulders. So, right then and there, standing in Pam's workshop, I struck a deal with the doggie gods. I promised to find a great groomer for Angel as soon as I got home. Given that I'm a crazed researcher, I figured that wouldn't be a challenge for me. Further, I committed myself to getting Angel into that groomer's shop once a month for the rest of her life in exchange for never having to go near a stripping comb for the rest of *my* life.

This bargain proved to be a spectacular success. My dog always looked gorgeous. And the comb is continuing to gather dust in my kitchen junk drawer even as I write this.

We emerged from Pam's grooming room with a miniature version of Rose. As Pam put her on the floor, I looked into the black-and-white face. Fluffy from the dryer, she gave me a fleeting glance, yawned, then pounced on a stuffed green dinosaur near my feet.

Humans can be so boring. Stuffed toys are much more fun. Besides which, you're way too intense right now. Even with Jigger helping you. Look, I know this is a big moment for you. After all, you're going to be taking me home with you. It doesn't get any more special than that.

Actually, I'm kinda glad you understand how big a deal this is.

But...geesh. Could you lighten up? Just a bit?

I'll think I'll ignore you for a while. Maybe you'll get the point and relax.

So much for my fantasy of the one true dog of my dreams pressed to my side forever. This beast wasn't even interested in me.

Panic reemerged. What if she didn't like me? What if she never liked me? I'd just spent seventeen years with a cat who barely came out from under the bed except to eat her much-loved tuna. I couldn't stand to be ignored by another pet. Damn it! I wanted a dog who would shower me with undying devotion and affection, who would be at my heels every moment.

I heard myself mutter, "Wow. The toy has her complete attention. It's like we're not even here."

Pam grinned. "English cockers know what they want. And they'll accept little else. You'll get used to it."

Somehow, I doubted it.

My thoughts continued to drift into negative territory. What if we couldn't get her housetrained? What if she continued to ignore us? What kind of nightmare had we created for ourselves?

Pam broke into my thoughts with her usual brusqueness. "Grab your leash. Time to go."

Angel abandoned her toy without a trace of reluctance. She accepted her end of the leash with another yawn, her nonchalance balancing my nerves.

Are we going now, or what?

I turned to Pam. "Does she want to take the toy with her? We'd be happy to buy it from you."

She chuckled and pointed down to Angel, who had started to walk toward the door within the limits of the leash. "Doesn't look like she really cares about it, does it?"

I looked back at Jigger as Angel led us to the door. That inscrutable grin of hers was plastered on her face. And then, she winked at me. Yes, I'm sure she winked at me. Then she turned away and walked from the room. Her job was done. The hand-off had occurred. Angel had taken her place.

For her part, Angel was the picture of calm confidence. She trotted by our sides as if she'd done so a million times. She didn't bat an eyelash at the strange car. She hopped onto my lap without a second's hesitation. I looked down at her, thinking either this dog was dumb as a brick and didn't have a clue what was going on, or she was incredibly secure and accepted the novelty as if it were nothing.

Yes, I realize you've read enough to know immediately which scenario was the case. I, on the other hand, needed many experiences with her before I truly understood the steadiness of this dog.

After a vague wave from Pam, we started the car and rumbled down her driveway to the road. Minutes later, we were speeding along the expressway, Michigan farmhouses and cultivated corn fields flashing by us. We were still a few hours from the urban grit of Chi-town.

I heaved a sigh—a combination of relief, weariness, and nervousness. The warm ball of fluff sprawled across my thighs sighed, too.

So tired. I've had a very busy day.

Her even, deep breathing told me she'd fallen asleep again. I looked at the downy black-and-white baby, her breaths now coming in short puffs in sync with twitching front paws as she dreamed. A surge of affection overwhelmed me, and tears filled my eyes. The image of Jigger faded. This slumbering pooch was *ours*, and in that moment—and every one afterward—she filled my world.

I studied the four-month-old body. Long black ears framed an aristocratic narrow head that was marked with a wide strip of speckled white traveling down its center. Two perfectly symmetrical stretches of black drifted from the white strip to the top of her ears. Fuzzy white-and-black fur cascaded down well-formed legs and paws. A pair of large black patches sprawled across her shoulders. They vaguely resembled the shape of wings, probably the markings that differentiated her from her litter mates and the reason Pam had called her "Angel."

Angel. I hated the name. But I'd reconciled to it, assuming we were stuck with it since that's what she'd been called from birth. Until I brought up the subject with Pam, who brushed off my concern. "She'll recognize any damn thing anyone who feeds her wants to use. This breed is obsessed with food. Pick whatever name you like. She won't have a problem adjusting to it as long as her dish is full."

And so our slumbering dog completely missed a lively debate over her name.

"Boomer," my husband supplied.

"You're kidding…right?"

He merely smiled at me, and I realized he was serious.

"Umm, maybe not." I said this with some delicacy, trying not to hurt his feelings. I thought longingly of the myriad of websites devoted to pet names. I vaguely remembered compiling a sheet of possible candidates, but God knows where that was in the chaos of my notes.

"What about some obscure name from a Shakespearean play, or from the movies, or something like that?" I ventured. "You know, a bit of style and uniqueness."

"How many dogs do you know called Boomer?"

"Marc!"

Chuckling, he replied, "I'm just sayin'…"

"Ophelia?"

"Please! And no 'Juliet,' either."

"So forget Shakespeare. What about a movie star? Or the name of a place?" Glancing out the car window, I noticed a mileage marker for Kalamazoo, Michigan.

Kalamazoo…Kala…Mazoo…Kal…

"Oh, my God, that's it! 'Callie.'" I sat upright, nearly toppling the puppy onto the floor. Forgetting my moment of inspiration, I studied her to see if she was awake. She shifted position on my lap, never opening her eyes.

"That's not bad," Marc said, thoughtfully. "Not bad at all. How do you want to spell it?"

"C-A-L-L-I-E, of course."

"Boring. What about K-A-L-L-I?"

I sighed. At least we hadn't been stuck with "Boomer."

"Sold," I replied.

Marc glanced at the sleeping baby and added, "Have you ever seen such a well-adjusted, secure little animal?"

His words were more accurate than he could have known in that moment. It quickly became clear to us that Kalli was exactly as he had described her, thanks in large part to solid, healthy bloodstock and a gifted breeder.

Our job was simple. All we had to do was not screw her up.

WELCOME HOME

With a towering stack of puppy-training books hovering by the landing, Marc and I opened the side door and brought Kalli into the air-conditioned stillness of her new home. A gust of steamy heat from the late afternoon whooshed into the galley kitchen ahead of us.

We'd decided our puppy should be trained to stop just inside the house when coming in from outside so we could always wipe off her paws. Okay, so maybe it was my idea and Marc had agreed to go along with me. Still, it was an excellent practice, I told myself as I stopped Kalli from bounding into the house. With heartfelt authority, my voice rang out. "Kalli, paws."

She looked up at me as if I was out of my mind.

You have got to be kidding. What kind of lunatic are you, anyway? Here I am...a wretched, pathetic baby, tragic over the loss of my mom and litter mates. Suffering from...what do you humans call it? Oh, yeah. Separation Anxiety. And you want to start training me? Honey, the only thing you can expect from me right now are well-placed poops on your Oriental carpet and piddles on the kitchen floor.

I ignored her attitude. It was important I establish my alpha role. I knew that was true because I'd read it in a book.

Suddenly feeling naked without my research, I wondered where that book was, exactly. Buried deep in the teetering stack by the kitchen door? Yup. It was the one from which tons of red paper strips stuck out. I'd color-coded my bookmarks, you see. And red noted particularly significant passages.

No time for the book, now. I grabbed a small towel I'd left by the door and rubbed Kalli's dry and perfectly clean paws. The books said to be consistent.

I could have sworn she rolled her eyes at me. I know for a fact her eyebrows raised in a particularly disdainful way. This was a gavotte of behavior and attitude she and I would dance zillions of times in the years ahead, and over much more than her paws.

The cleansing portion of her welcome home ritual accomplished, Kalli waited for the leash to be unsnapped before she darted through the kitchen and disappeared into the dining room at breakneck speed. Her tracking instincts were in full bloom and she had new territory to explore.

So much for our peaceful, slumbering puppy.

Out of the corner of my eye, I saw her circle the oval dining table for the third time. I headed for the books and reams of notes, already suffering withdrawal from my information addiction. Hadn't I prepared a special page of notes for just this moment? Something about "introducing your new puppy to your house." With frantic jerks, I rifled through one stack of paper, then another. Damn. Not there. Not anywhere.

Okay, which book talked about this? And what had it said? Were you supposed to keep the leash on and introduce the environment to your puppy bit by bit? No, wait. That was if you already had animals in the household and you were introducing them. No, that wasn't right, either. If you had other pets, you were supposed to introduce the newcomer on neutral ground and not in the house at all—

Wait a minute. We didn't have other pets.

All the while, Kalli was having a fine time exploring, witnessed by Marc, who had wisely ignored my papers and books and had decided to enjoy the experience of a new puppy without professional input. To my credit, I joined him in the sunroom, leaving my research behind. All right, maybe I did have a teensy volume still clamped in my hand, but I ignored it as I entered the bright room at the back of the house.

Our new addition had worked her way through towering pots of tropical plants to climb onto our white couch. Grinning from ear to ear, she ranged back and forth from one end to the other, nose buried in the upholstery.

"We really shouldn't allow her to—"

Marc cut me off with a wave of his hand. "Let her look around."

Right. He was right. Forget what the books would say about this clear act of testing.

I watched Kalli in action. Her stub tail erect with excitement, her butt wiggling a mile a minute, she was pure joy in motion. To hell with the book.

That evening, I once again dragged out my tomes. Information addiction is a tough nut to crack. And with no twelve-step program available, I was on my own to cope with it. I didn't even try to resist. Soon, my nose was buried between the pages as I reviewed how to prepare your puppy for her first night.

Set up the crate. Check.

Position the crate so it's out of drafts and traffic lanes. Check.

Create a comfy nest of towels and stuffed toys. Check. And let's not forget those tastefully matching bumpers I'd selected.

It was time to put the baby to bed.

With great ceremony, Marc and I roused our exhausted puppy from her bolster bed by our living room coffee table. We snapped on her leash and prepared to escort her outside for her "last" potty of the day. Of course, the books had warned us that a puppy might well need many trips to the yard throughout the night, but we decided to be optimistic.

We'd designated a corner by the side of the house as her potty area and that's where we headed. Kalli had other ideas. All traces of sleepiness gone, she pulled at the leash, heading for every strange shadow she could find that wasn't in the target area. She seemed especially obsessed with the back area by the garage.

The books had said to be firm about trips outside with a dog still in the process of being housetrained. Until the animal could be trusted to tell you when she needed to go, she shouldn't be allowed to be in the yard except for her business. And then only in the spot chosen by the human for that business.

Kalli hadn't read the book.

"Kalli, go potty!" I spoke in firm tones. Marc raised an eyebrow. I nodded. "That's the command. Both of us need to use it."

"I know." He waved a weary hand through the sultry evening air. "We're supposed to be consistent."

"Exactly." I repeated the command to our puppy, and I could almost feel her scorn drifting toward us on the hot wind.

"She does have an attitude, doesn't she?" Marc laughed softly.

Again his words foretold the future. Kalli's "attitude" would become legendary.

After a bit more coaxing, we accomplished our mission—in the correct spot. I started to escort her toward the house. She stopped in her tracks and stared at me.

Okay, I did what you asked. Turnabout is fair play. Can't I sniff around, just a little? Puppies need to have fun, you know. It's important for you to provide a balanced environment for me so my delicate nature can evolve in a healthy manner.

What? You're not buying that? Hmmm, you may be smarter than you seem. Okay, ditch the logic. Let's appeal to your emotions. If I give you my particularly cute, endearing look, just maybe...

I paused, studying her.

"What?" Marc had walked to the side door, then turned back when he realized we weren't behind him.

I shrugged. "I don't know. Maybe we should ignore the book and let her wander around the yard a bit." His satire of a shocked expression made me giggle. "Well, the impossible does happen," I added in a weak voice.

I looked into Kalli's eyes, barely visible in our yard light. "I have a feeling she's going to be training us more than we're going to be training her." And with total rebellion against everything I'd researched, I unsnapped her lead and let her roam the modest space.

"You're in trouble with trainers everywhere!" I warmed to Marc's gentle humor and arm around my shoulders.

The soft breeze captured the aroma of blooming shrub roses edging the patio, sending it to us in gauzy wisps. An owl hooted from the forest greenbelt a few blocks away. The golden glow of our neighbor's table lamp by their kitchen window stamped the ground at our feet.

Marc and I stood together, arm-in-arm, watching our English cocker streak in and out of the shadows. The patch of periwinkle around the giant honey locust tree particularly captured her attention, as did the tree itself.

"If she could climb that tree, she'd be halfway up by now," Marc said in my ear.

I nodded, watching Kalli stretch her front paws up the trunk as far as she could reach, then hold them there as her hind legs bounced her around the circumference of the venerable tree. I thought of the steady traffic of squirrels up and down that bark every day and understood our tracking dog was hard at work.

"Wonder what she'll do when she sees one of our squirrels?" I mused.

"That's entertainment!"

Suddenly, she darted away, heading for the back corner that had fascinated her minutes before. Raucous barking followed, and we hurried toward her. We arrived just in time to see Kalli push her way behind the wire-enclosed compost pile, in hot pursuit of—

I caught the flashing shadow of a small animal as it squeezed between the fence pickets and ran out into the alley. A white stripe on its back blazed in light from nearby street lamps.

"Skunk!" I yelled, diving for Kalli. I snatched the surprised dog and wheeled around for the house like a receiver protecting a game-winning ball from the defensive line. I'd only made it halfway to the side door when the stench descended.

I picked up my speed and hurtled into the house. I didn't even think about going through the paw-wiping ritual.

"Did it spray her?" Marc was hot on my heels.

"I don't think so. Close the door."

We stopped in the middle of the kitchen floor with Kalli squirming in my arms.

Give me a break. I was just starting to have fun. I can't believe you two stopped me. This is not what I meant when I mentioned that balance thing a few minutes ago.

The stink oozed around us, carried on the tiniest bit of outside air that had invaded our house.

"You sure it didn't get her?" Marc sniffed at Kalli, who happily licked his face when it came close to her muzzle. "Nope. She's okay. That smell is general, not concentrated on her."

"Thank God!" I breathed the words. "I can't imagine how awful it would have been if that thing had gotten her. You know how hard it is to get the smell out of fur? Remember Taj?" I referred to our friends' Samoyed, who had been attacked by a skunk in the wilds of Wisconsin when they were on vacation a few years before. While his owners had managed to clean him at the time, they'd had to deal with his fur smelling faintly of skunk whenever it got wet for months afterward. In our case, little did I know we'd have more encounters with Evanston's skunk population in the years ahead.

The wriggling dog reminded me I'd held on to her way too long. Kalli was never one to be carried, or to curl up on a lap, for that matter.

"We've had enough excitement for today. Let's get her to bed." Marc grabbed the leash I'd draped across my shoulders and snapped it on her collar. "She might not be tired, but I'm exhausted."

Together, the three of us marched to the stairs leading to our second-floor bedroom. Only to be stopped in our tracks. Kalli had frozen in place at the bottom of the stairway.

"What?" I asked her.

She crept forward, sniffing the bottom step, then stretching her neck to its limits to sniff the next one.

"I don't think she knows how to climb stairs." Marc spoke behind me.

"How can that be? Pam traveled with her all over the place. And Kalli lived in the house with her."

"A one-story house."

"That's right!" Further, I realized we'd limited Kalli's exploration of our house to an area away from the stairway. This was the first time she'd been in this portion of our home. I looked down and watched her react to the situation.

She glanced at me over her shoulder.

Oh, geesh. She's worried about me.

Look, honey, I'll figure this out. Just relax. I love challenges. Besides, there are new smells up there and I am not a dog to ever turn down the opportunity to explore fresh ground...so to speak.

Her nose extended a bit higher on the stairway, and she carefully planted her front paws on the bottom step. The nose, like a periscope seeking a new depth, moved up the next step. Front paws scooted forward, but resisted moving up along with it. That would have required the rear legs to climb the stairs. It seemed Kalli was not quite ready to do that.

"Should we help her?" Marc asked.

A wave of powerlessness swept over me. Longingly, I looked at the nearest stack of doggie books perched on the front hall table. I was sure the answer would be in there. But I didn't want to leave my post by Kalli's side. Instinct told me to stay in place.

"Let's see if she can work it through on her own."

Attention returning to my dog, I watched her lift one rear paw and place it on the next step up. Then the other rear paw. She paused and looked at us from her great height.

Ha!! Told you. Never underestimate a spaniel.

In the same tentative fashion, she moved up to the next step, and up one more. Then she threw caution to the wind. Front paws up...rear paws up...front...rear... By the time she reached the landing, she was moving at a good clip. After clearing the landing, she raced the rest of the way, screeching to a halt on the second floor with a wide grin on her face. She didn't need to say a thing. Her expression communicated all.

"All right, kid," Marc said to her. "Going up is one thing, but can you come down?"

Of course I can. No problem. See? I'm doing it now. Right now. One paw out... Hmmm... Really, I can do this. You just watch. I'm about to start. Yup, this very instant. No more hesitating. I'm on it. Er... Uh...

Okay, so maybe I need the teensiest bit of help. I am just a puppy, after all.

Marc joined her at the top of the stairs, then began to descend, turning back to her. "Let's go. Let's see if you can do it."

With calm determination, she lowered her muzzle and sniffed out the situation. I was learning that Kalli's tracking instincts surged in her blood and her solution to most dilemmas was to apply her nose to them. She extended her muzzle out into space over the stairs and almost tumbled forward. Beating a hasty retreat to the level surface of the second floor, she reevaluated her position.

Marc patted the step immediately below the floor. "Come on, sweetheart. You can do this. Just take it easy."

The withering look she tossed him would have wilted a lesser man, but Marc just chuckled and waited for her. He had clearly thrown down a spaniel gauntlet.

I was about to learn that Kalli was never one to back away from a challenge. With concentrated effort, she dropped her front paws down one step...and stopped. I thought I saw a bit of panic cross her eyes.

Umm...so far so good. I'm good. Really. No problem...

Marc started back up the steps toward her, and his implied support was all the impetus she seemed to need to get moving. The rear paws dropped behind the front paws on the step, and though her legs appeared a bit shaky to me, she resolutely soldiered on. Front paws lowered to the next level and her hind end followed a bit more quickly than it had previously.

Her momentum picked up as she continued her descent. It would take another few days of experimentation before she achieved the fast, controlled fall that would became her modus operandi throughout most of her life.

Down in the front hall once again, Kalli seized the opportunity to demonstrate her new skill. Whirling around she raced up the stairs, then tore back down, paws a blur, ears flying, grin widening. On the main floor once again, she tore throughout the rooms in a victory lap before attacking the stairs like a seasoned pro and making her way to the upstairs hallway in a relaxed sprint. Tongue lolling to one side, she panted with happy abandon as she began her exploration of our second floor.

Marc and I looked at each other, relieved that the stairway episode had gone so well. "You know," I said to him in a soft voice, "now that I think about it, I don't remember any of my books tackling the subject of stairs."

He laughed and wrapped his arms around me, placing a gentle kiss on my cheek. "I just bet they don't. And see how well we did."

I nodded. "All on our own." Perhaps I didn't need the books after all.

I held to that thought until we entered the bedroom with Kalli. Then uncertainty struck me again. What would Kalli's reaction be to her first night in a strange house, in a strange crate? Sure, she seemed calm now, but what about after the door latched shut? Would we be forced to endure heartbroken puppy cries until morning?

In a panic, I wracked my brain, trying to remember what my books claimed was the proper method for introducing the little one to a new crate.

"Uh, Laura?" Marc nodded toward the far end of our bedroom, a big grin on his face.

I looked over to see he'd unsnapped the leash, and Kalli was already inside the kennel. She circled three times, flopped onto her towel nest with a contented sigh, and shut her eyes.

Marc latched the crate door, and I held my breath.

Kalli opened an eye, looked in his direction, then closed it with another sigh. I could have sworn she winked at him. A few minutes later, her gentle snores filled the quiet room.

The little bugger slept through the night as if she didn't have a care in the world. Until her last few months of life, she spent every night of her years with us in exactly the same way.

PAELLA...SPANIEL STYLE

Kalli's arrival coincided with Fourth of July weekend. We'd worried about our puppy freaking out with the firework celebration that was traditional in our neighborhood. It frayed my nerves every year. I couldn't imagine a young dog adjusting to a new home taking it in stride. I'd even tried to delay picking her up from her breeder's house to avoid this scene, but Pam's schedule hadn't permitted it.

In response to my worry, she'd answered me in her usual brusque fashion. "She'll look to you and Marc to see if there's some reason for concern. If you two take the noise in stride, so will she."

Yup. We had the quintessential secure puppy on our hands, courtesy of this brisk lady. And the holiday event unfolded exactly as Pam had described it. The three of us lounged on the patio when the first firecrackers boomed into the still-light summer sky. Kalli turned to us in question.

What is that?

We smiled at her, and I said, "It's okay, Kalli. Just a bit of noise. It can't hurt you." And I went back to my book and pretended to resume reading as if nothing was going on.

Out of the corner of my eye, I saw her stare at me for a few moments, eyebrows flicking. Then she shifted focus to a ladybug creeping across the patio tiles.

Oh, geesh. They're really worried about me. Ho hum. I can use this reaction of theirs to my benefit. All I have to do is figure out how.

Maybe later. Right now it's boring me. And I hate being bored. Makes me downright sleepy. I'm going to close my eyes and have me a nap.

Hey! You stupid little crawling thing. You bumped my paw. What are you, anyway? You look kinda worthless. I wonder if you taste good.

"She's really something, isn't she?" I could hear admiration in Marc's words.

"Couldn't agree more."

The fireworks crisis behind us, we faced down the challenge of housetraining. Kalli didn't seem even remotely interested in pottying outside. We received the distinct impression she found the whole process unimportant and beneath her.

Back to the books…no easy task since each expert recommended a unique training regimen for this aspect of civilizing our canine. One claimed the owner should *always* use newspapers with the new puppy. Another said you should *never* use newspapers. Someone else stressed that you should *rub* their noses in their mess should they slip in the house. *Never rub* their noses in the mess, came the opposing view— it's negative reinforcement that will only build resentment in your young dog. Another expert told me to *limit* the amount of water I should give Kalli so I could schedule her potty breaks. *No, don't ever limit* water, offered a different trainer. And so forth.

Overwhelmed with an embarrassment of riches in the information department, I picked a book at random and skimmed it. I remembered reading this material the month before and had been struck with its commonsense approach.

The author advised starting the process by calming the young animal in a crate for a short time, then taking it outside. If the baby pottied in the yard on a given trip, it was praised, given treats, and allowed an hour or so of "liberty"—play and exercise. If the puppy had not performed, it was to be returned to the kennel for fifteen to twenty minutes, then escorted to the potty area again. If the animal didn't respond appropriately, the process was repeated. And so on, until it understood the link between pottying and the outdoors.

Marc and I agreed with this strategy and started implementing it on Marc's birthday—the fifth of July. We decided to forego our usual fancy birthday dinner out and stay home. Leaving Kalli alone on her third day in a new place hadn't seemed kind or wise.

We opted to spend the day making Marc's favorite dish—paella— a complex recipe that took a zillion hours to do (albeit worth it when we sat down to eat the food). On this occasion, it proved to be a perfect daylong project. We could keep an eye on Kalli in her kitchen crate and cook the dish at the same time.

By late morning, our kitchen counter was overflowing. Packages of chicken and chorizo sat next to a bottle of wine. Vegetables joined the mix—onions, green peppers, peas, and tomatoes. Fresh seafood included sacks of fresh shrimp, clams, mussels, and scallops. A tiny glass bottle of pricey saffron lurked behind the pimento.

Kalli watched us assemble our ingredients through the grid of her crate door with interest.

Now we're talking. Food. Serious food. Man! It's all over the place. Way too much for the two of them. Although they look like they could eat it all if they wanted to.

Nah... There's gotta be something for me to munch on somewhere in that stuff.

But I can't even get at it. Here I am, stuck in this box thing and all because I haven't piddled yet. Not that I don't have to. I've been holding it forever! And yeah, I'm really uncomfortable, but it's so worth it...watching them scramble around to get me outside, begging me.

Working so darn hard at it. I thought Mommy was going to cry on her last trip with me. Hee...hee...hee...

I love it when they beg. They're so much fun!

I looked across the room in time to catch a fascinated expression on Kalli's face. "Does that look like a dog who's ready to potty?"

Marc shrugged. "Her last trip was fifteen minutes ago, and she didn't seem interested in it. She's still too busy hunting her skunk buddy."

"How long has it been since we last saw something exit her body?"

He consulted a meticulously maintained log on the counter. "Ummm...boy! Four hours! You'd think she'd have to go out by now."

"Yes, you'd think so."

We turned in unison to study her. She stared back and raised her eyebrows at us.

Yup. Too darn much fun.

I reached for the black leather leash hanging from a wall hook next to the side door. "I'll take her this time." I unlatched the crate door and grabbed Kalli's collar as she sensed freedom and started to bolt from the kitchen. "No such luck," I told her, snapping the leash onto her collar. "We're going out, kid."

Clearly happy to be going anywhere other than her kennel, Kalli bounced next to me, down the steps and sidewalk to the gate leading to our backyard. Let the wandering begin.

Our little dog had quickly mastered the fine art of sniffing every inch of her designated area with consummate concentration. We realized if we allowed it, her excruciatingly detailed scrutiny of every one-thousandth inch would keep her nose occupied for hours. Without a hint of a piddle or poop.

The secret of a successful outing was to give her the latitude to complete her business if she were so inclined, but not let her take advantage and spend her whole time exploring. This proved to be a delicate line of which Marc and I always seemed to be on the wrong side.

Indeed, the balancing act was an ongoing theme in our relationship with her throughout her life. No matter how determined we were to be fair and evenhanded, but not too permissive, Kalli managed to push the boundary in her favor. Eventually, we learned not to get upset about it. Frankly, watching her devious mind concoct complex scenarios designed to place us at a disadvantage was pure joy.

However, on that steamy July afternoon, I felt annoyed, not joyful.

Ha! Really getting to you, aren't I? Think I'll sniff the tip of this ivy leaf for the twentieth time.

"Kalli, come on! I have chicken sautéing in the pan."

Not my problem. 'Course, if you want to give me a taste…

I looked at my watch. The only way I could keep these outings positive, was to limit them to ten minutes. That was all my patience could handle of her snuffling.

Time up, I resolutely turned toward the house, my reluctant dog dragging her paws as she attempted to inhale each blade of grass along the sidewalk.

And thus continued the pattern of the day:

Sauté chicken. Take out Kalli. No piddle. No poop.

Brown the onion, pepper, and chorizo. Take out Kalli. No success.

Onions and peppers now tender. Take out Kalli. Minor piddle. No poop.

Add tomatoes and wine. Marc rewards Kalli.

Place saffron in rice, add to mixture, let it simmer. Take out Kalli. No piddle. No poop.

Pour stock into the rice. Take out Kalli yet again.

Still nothing.

The end of the day yielded a tiny poop, a giant pan of paella, and the scary belief that our dog could count and tell time.

Still, she never pottied inside the house from that moment until the last months of her life when her geriatric body betrayed her. We suspect she'd known all about housetraining the whole time, but played our game just so she could watch us jump through hoops of our very own making. She ended the game when she grew bored with it.

Such was life with Kalli.

OUT IN THE 'HOOD

Of course, the whole world knew about Kalli's impending arrival. At least, my version of the whole world. I'd been talking about little else for months before we picked her up at Pam's. Neighbors, friends, family were all primed for the big event. My sister had even offered to host a "baby" shower for me…her acknowledgement of all the money and time Marc and I had spent supporting our friends' and family members' babies without having a reciprocal gathering in our own household.

The first friends to encounter Kalli were old college chums with a seven-year-old son. We spent part of the holiday weekend at their house, figuring it was never too early to socialize our puppy. All the books claimed exposing a dog to a new environment broadened its horizon and enabled it to adjust to the "outside" world. It helped that Jerry and Taylor had a puppy-proof enclosed backyard, and the weather was picture perfect. Other than ripping up an ancient golf glove lodged under a drain pipe, Kalli was on her best behavior.

We also noticed magic beginning to build between our puppy and Billy. The little boy had fallen in love with Kalli at first sight. We suspected that Kalli's attraction to Billy centered on remnants of his latest meal that had eluded the parental damp cloth and still clung to his skin and clothes. Indeed, Billy's face became her prime target whenever she spotted him. But that was okay. It was a symbiotic relationship. Billy delighted in her attention; she delighted in his leftovers. The sound of her lapping tongue and his giggles still resonate in my head.

Our first turn around the 'hood didn't prove to be as idyllic as the afternoon in Jerry and Taylor's backyard. The walk started out well enough. Kalli accepted the leash with good humor and ate up the attention as neighbors exclaimed over her: "Oh, my God, is she cute! What breed is she?"

Thus was born my "English Cocker 101" speech. Throughout the years, I honed it to a fine point.

Marc and I felt our confidence build in this beautiful young dog with each step we took down the tree-lined sidewalk by our house. Cocky with our decision to adopt such an amazing animal, we were sure we'd won the I-Have-The-Best-Pet-In-The-World lottery. We exchanged smug glances as we noticed a friend approach on the other side of the street with his beagle, Sam.

Eager to show off our wonderful canine, we had just begun to cross the street toward them when a God-awful shriek slammed through the steamy July air. It was the agony-filled scream of someone being dismembered, the nightmare squeal as millions of fingernails ripped across thousands of blackboards, the excruciating wail as boiling oil cascaded on barbarians storming the castle gates. It was…

…our dog.

Specifically, this was our dog looking at a non-English cocker. Had our perfect little pet ever been around a canine other than one from her own breed?

HELP! HELP! What is that? I've never seen anything like it. It's the ugliest whatever it is. How could such a beast be allowed to exist? HELP!!

We froze, staring at Kalli in horror. Sam cowered behind his owner's legs.

Neighbors rushed to their windows and doors, sure that some pathetic animal was being tortured. Their glares said it all: What are you doing to that sweet little thing? Do we need to call the police?

We dropped beside Kalli and tried to calm her. Only when Sam had left her line of sight did she stop caterwauling. Then, she resumed the walk in blessed silence as if nothing had happened. From our peripheral vision, we saw folks move back into their houses with a final angry look tossed our direction. For our part, we wondered if dogs could be schizophrenic.

Pam responded to our frantic phone call. "Yes, I meant to warn you about that. Not all my dogs do that, of course. But some of them are very breed-sensitive. Looks like Kalli is one of those."

No kidding. I looked over my shoulder to watch my puppy chewing a small rawhide stick with complete enjoyment and concentration. I was still trying to figure out how such a tiny beast could make such a huge racket.

Returning my attention to the phone, I said, "So, what do we do about it?"

"Expose her to as many dogs as you can."

"But—"

"Make certain you and Marc greet the other dog as if nothing is wrong. Once she sees you're interested in it, she'll be curious and jealous as hell. After this happens a few times, she'll forget all about carrying on. Trust me."

As usual, Pam was right...eventually. It took more than a few encounters with non-spaniels before the anguished howling stopped.

Kalli greeted our human neighbors in a much quieter fashion. They owned cats.

Ron and Maddie were sitting on their patio a few days after our Paella Housetraining Event when I took out Kalli for an afternoon exploration of the yard.

Ron called to me. "Is that the baby? Look at that puppy wuppy!"

Kalli sensed the appreciate audience and her butt began wiggling as she trotted to the fence.

Maddie trilled, "Oh, my God! Is she the cutest thing you've ever seen, or what?"

Kalli's butt wiggled harder and a grin spread across her face.

Now these are my kind of people. Talk about easy marks. I bet I could get them to do anything. Yup. Anything.

Except...

...where's the challenge? I've won them over without even trying. Frankly, this is kinda boring. Although if they want to pet me, I guess I could manage to give them a few minutes of my time.

Kalli jumped up against the pickets as Ron and Maddie reached over the fence to stroke her fur. Soon, their hands were slathered with puppy goo as she licked them with fierce concentration.

I watched the exchange of pure delight moving from one side of the fence to the other and captured the moment in my heart. This was what having a dog was all about.

Taking a deep breath, I reflected on the beauty of the day, and everyone agreed Evanston in July was a great place to be. I heard a June bug buzzing under the shrubs, and Ron noted it was a "month off."

Kalli dropped away from the fence and trotted to the shrubs. Suddenly, the insect's racket was muffled. I turned in time to see Kalli shimmy out from under the bush. As she approached me, the bug's muted call grew a bit louder.

An expression in her eyes set off warning bells. She was attempting to look nonchalant.

Too nonchalant.

"Uh, Laura? I think she has that June bug in her mouth." Maddie giggled.

Sure enough, the sound was coming from behind Kalli's clenched jaw.

"You might want to get that away from her."

Barely noticing Ron's somber tones, I had already grasped Kalli's jaws with one hand and jimmied her mouth open with the other. The bug sprinted out and disappeared in a huff, its raucous complaints growing fainter with distance.

"Good work!"

Now, I recognized his uncharacteristic seriousness. "What?"

Ron shook his head. "Just not envying you. Puppies put everything in their mouths."

Maddie jumped in. "Now don't you go scaring Laura with horror stories. Even your dogs managed to survive puppyhood."

He smiled at her. "You're absolutely right, honey. I worry too much. They all grew up just fine, didn't they?" Then he waved a hand in Kalli's direction. "Still, I'm betting this one'll be a handful. She looks particularly adventurous."

I swept my puppy into my arms, much to her frustration. She had begun to stalk a robin hopping across our rose bed.

What is your problem? I'm busy here.

"Oh, Kalli. We have to keep you safe!" I buried my head in the fur around her neck. Her squirming didn't allow the moment to continue. "Yeah, yeah, I know. You have other places to be!"

She shook herself.

Damn straight I do! You really take things much too seriously, you know that? Life is about fun and taking chances. If you never explore and try new stuff, how can you learn?

I caught the look and knew she was telling me to lighten up. And while I never pulled anything dangerous from her mouth in the years ahead, she did manage to munch on the most disgusting things. Goose poop and a decomposed baby bird top my list.

WHO NEEDS TO BE SOCIAL?

Marc and I had lined up a dog trainer as soon as we'd identified Kalli's breeder and knew we had a puppy coming. As it turned out, I was spared laborious research into the matter when my therapist identified a trainer for whom her daughter worked.

Kristen was a marvel. The right person at the right time. Her no-nonsense approach was tempered by a healthy dose of humor and kindly instinct. Most important, she had Kalli's number the moment she met her.

She entered our house with an easy smile and eyes on our dog. Kalli, always the consummate hostess, wiggled her butt to the max and dove into the oversized bag Kristen casually slung to the floor. Trying to present myself as the responsible owner, I immediately chastised her. I received a baleful canine eye and a chuckle from the trainer.

"Nothing in there to worry about. My bags are always puppy-proofed."

"But—"

She shook her head. "We'll get to the training, soon. Right now, just let her be a baby."

This wasn't what I'd expected. I was prepared to launch into intensive training sessions, tackling the lofty commands, "sit," "stay," "down." But when I verbalized this, she chuckled again. "Nope. The important thing now is to socialize her as much as possible and let her be goofy for the next month or so. My beginning obedience class begins in the fall. We'll start serious work then. In the meantime, you can teach her 'sit' if you'd like." She proceeded to show us how to lower Kalli's butt to the floor, and left us with a wave and "See you in September" drifting on the July air.

Marc winked at me. "Let me guess. Too casual for you?"

I batted his arm. "Nice." And proceeded to teach my dog her first command in five minutes.

Socializing her wasn't as easy. "Try a doggie play group," Maddie suggested. "There's a bunch of folks who meet after work at a park a few blocks away. I bet they'd love to have this cutie join them." She leaned over and scratched Kalli behind the ears, receiving a fierce butt wiggle in response.

I loved Maddie's idea. We could meet new friends—canine and human—and nurture Kalli at the same time. I looked down at her. She'd flopped on her back so Maddie could scratch her tummy. It was time our little girl expanded her social circle.

Marc and I researched the group and located the contact person. I grilled the poor man, working off a sheet overflowing with carefully chosen questions. All answers were satisfactory. Especially important to me were two items: aggressive dogs were weeded out of the group, and the recreational field on which they played was surrounded by a safety fence.

Perfect. But just to make certain the venue's "i's" were dotted and "t's" crossed, I called Kristen and explained the setup to her.

"Sounds great," she said in a brisk voice.

"But she doesn't know a proper recall," I said, throwing out one of my undotted "i's."

"Of course that would be ideal, and she'll learn the 'come' command soon enough. But it doesn't sound like she'll need it. She's safely fenced in. Besides which, she'll stick with the rest of the dogs since that's where the fun is. Right now, you just want her to socialize. Go. Enjoy."

And with this official sanction from the expert, I made a date to present Kalli to the group at their next get-together.

The steamy July evening of our play date didn't impress my diva. She had revealed herself to be a true heat wimp from the first week she'd been with us. Once the temps topped eighty, walking her became a major challenge. Kalli would humor us for fifteen minutes or so, then stake her claim under a leafy tree and sprawl on the cool grass, drilling us with disdainful eyes brimming with her displeasure. If we elected to continue the walk, we received her patented raised eyebrows.

You really think I'm moving when it's this hot? Hmmph! Race down that path yourself and let me know how it feels. I'm staying here.

Marc eyed the thermometer as we prepared Kalli for her first true social occasion. "Do you know how hot it is out there?"

"No, and I don't want you to tell me. Especially with you-know-who listening." We were sure Kalli understood everything we said and were almost to the point of spelling key words.

We encouraged her out of the air-conditioned house, promising more air conditioning in the car and liver treats as baits. Once at the park, we urged her from the car with a healthy dose of threats…and more treats. She sighed as we pushed open the gate to the soccer field and strolled onto the grass.

The leash radiated with Kalli's reaction to the scene before her. I swear her every muscle froze. Before us raced a bunch of pooches numbering twenty or so…of all breeds and sizes.

Oh…My…God.

This has to be hell. Pure hell. It was bad enough when I had Mama Pam's brats running around her yard. At least they were like me. Of course, they weren't as amazing as I am. How many dogs are? But this!

This is...well, I don't know if I have a word for it...which in and of itself is remarkable.

I can't believe there are so many ill-mannered brutes in one place. They're...they're barbarians. I don't know what Mommy and Daddy expect me to do with...them. Maybe I'm just here to observe...something to shock me into appreciating my new life with these two humans. I mean, they aren't that bad when all is said and done. And at least I don't have to contend with other dogs.

Okay, I give. Yes, I truly appreciate them. Yes, I love my new life. Now...can I leave? Please????

"What do you think is about to happen?" Marc said in my ear.

I shrugged. "Only one way to find out." Our puppy was still in frozen mode, broken by a few quick backward steps as a golden retriever raced toward her to make friends.

"Baby Doll! Come here this instant!" warbled a blue-haired diminutive lady in a fuzzy pink warm-up suit.

The golden tossed a toothy grin over its shoulder at her, then moved in to sniff Kalli.

"I mean it!" she insisted, her voice elevating an octave. Much higher and only the animals could have heard her. Baby Doll didn't even bother to look at her this time.

Marc and I watched the golden inspect Kalli and waited for spaniel shrieking. I even closed my eyes, bracing myself.

The only sound was that of the golden's happy panting. Taking a deep breath, I opened one eye to see the pair touching noses.

So you're not so bad. And you're very polite. Not that I want to play with you, of course.

"Oh my God," murmured Marc. "Will wonders never cease?"

"This may just work out great!"

I had spoken too soon. Obviously Baby Doll had sent out a silent alert, because the whole pack began converging on our position. I use the military metaphor because I really did feel invaded. Doggie enthusiasm is unparalleled when there's a stranger afoot. Canines swarmed around us, dripping tongues and tails everywhere.

Kalli shrank against my leg, then tried to climb it as wet noses were thrust at every inch of her. I picked her up and cradled her in my arms.

Now safely out of range of everyone but the tallest dogs, she started barking at the assemblage.

Heathens! All of you!! I have never! No, never!!! This is the most despicable...the most disgusting display...

Well, if I didn't know why I'm a people dog and not a doggie dog before, I certainly do now! Shoo! Shoo!!!

"Okay, knock it off! Give the kid a break," an authoritative male voice rang out.

As if auditioning for the Radio City Music Hall Rockettes, the entire pack turned on a dime, legs flying, and streamed toward the center of the field in flawless unison.

"Whoa," Marc said in a half-whistle. "Now that's someone who knows his stuff."

"I wouldn't want to cross him." I examined my dog. She looked none the worse for wear. I set her on the ground.

"Come on over!" hailed a third voice...this one youthful and female. "Join us. I can't wait to meet that darling thing of yours."

Searching for the one who'd called out this invitation, I spotted a young woman in khaki shorts and white T-shirt hugging an Irish setter.

Marc and I glanced at each other and shrugged. We'd survived thus far. In for a penny...

By this point, Kalli was pulling the leash toward a patch of shade at the edge of the field. I tugged back. "Nope. We're going this way. I know, you're not crazy about the idea, but that's the way it goes, kid. Buck up and try to enjoy yourself."

You mean to tell me you're really serious about this? Okay, I've done a lot for you folks so far. But enough is enough. Sometimes, a dog has to put a paw down and take her stand. And that's exactly what I'm doing. Holding my ground. Right here. Right now. I will not waste my time with these thugs.

I was prepared to ignore her dirty look. But I still had to get her to move. She'd settled in the shade the moment I stopped yanking the leash. It didn't appear she had any plans to budge.

"Hey, you." I turned on her and stood in front of her. Her eyes reluctantly met mine. "I can carry you over there as if you were a baby. Or you can walk like the awesome dog you are. Your choice." I ignored my inner voice telling me I had just mimicked, almost word for word, the speech I'd heard a mom give her toddler at the playground earlier that week.

In the end, Kalli deigned to accompany us toward the thicket of humans and canines. The animals started toward her again and the Voice thundered, "Noooooo!" They wheeled off to begin a lively game of tag farther down the field. Meanwhile, the Voice muttered, "Now, where did I put those balls?"

I located the speaker. A pasty, bald-headed man hovered over a cavernous canvas bag sitting on the ground, digging through it with vicious intent. This unassuming man provided my first inkling about the qualities necessary to handle dogs. Physical appearance, size, and girth, appeared *not* to be the key. Rather, dogs instinctively recognized humans who projected themselves as a leader figure, or alpha. After all, canines are pack animals. Their survival in the wild depends upon identifying and respecting the boss. They honor these same qualities in us.

I glanced at Kalli, wondering whether or not she saw me as alpha. "Yeah, right," I said under my breath as I guided her toward the Irish setter lady. Marc and I had a long way to go before either one of us came close to earning that status, I suspected. Although we had created the nickname for Marc, "Alpha Dad." It had been meant as a joke. But quickly, it had turned into a term of affection we were to use throughout Kalli's life.

"Oh, my!" oozed Ms. Irish setter. "Isn't she the sweetest thing you ever saw?"

Sweet? Kalli? "She does look the part, doesn't she?" I managed, positioning her so the woman could pet her.

She released her Irish setter, Artie, who couldn't have cared less about us. The mahogany beauty was soon lost in the crush of romping dogs.

"Now, what breed is she?"

We were soon fielding questions that gave me the opportunity to further evolve my English Cocker 101 speech. For her part, Kalli was perfectly content to allow this woman to appreciate her. Basking in Ellen's compliments, our little beast was never happier.

"Well, I've monopolized her too long," Ellen trilled. "You came here to let her play, not waste her time with me all evening." She rose and looked at us expectantly.

Ummmm. Marc and I exchanged glances. Did we want to force our little dog to go into that throng?

"Aren't you going to let her go?"

Irritation began to mount. Ellen was becoming downright pushy.

"Absolutely," I said through gritted teeth, unhooking the leash. Kalli set off at a confident trot. In the opposite direction from everyone else.

"What the—?"

I recognized her target immediately. How could I not? It was as plain as the nose on my face. A van had parked in a space on the road next to the field, its sliding doors wide open. No big deal. Kalli couldn't get to the street…except…

The moment I saw that break in the fence, shock waves hit me. "I thought this place was supposed to be completely enclosed," I hissed to Marc.

"That's what they said."

"Oh, it is for the most part," Ellen said in an airy tone. "There's only a single gap, but the dogs never pay any attention to it."

Maybe *those* dogs didn't. But *my* dog sure would.

I broke out in a run, chasing the stubby spaniel tail at top speed. I heard Marc first call my name, then take off after me.

Meanwhile, with the unerring precision of a guided missile, Kalli followed a straight line to the van…and the one-and-only gap in the fence.

We were no match for a motivated puppy. She passed the fence and bounded into the vehicle with happy abandon before we could close in on her. Adult laughter and gleeful baby squeals floated from the van.

Kalli had hit her target.

We skidded to a stop at the doors, staring at the scene before us. Kalli had hopped up on the seat next to an infant carrier and a gurgling baby. Her long pink tongue slurped the baby's cheeks.

"That's one way to clean her face."

I looked toward the speaker, a chuckling young woman in the driver's seat, hands submerged in a diaper bag.

"Oh, I'm so sorry," I sputtered.

She waved me off with an airy gesture. "Please. We're totally into dogs. My husband's out there with our Lab. Tessa's been fussy ever since they hit the field, so anything that can entertain her is very welcome."

"Yes, but the germs." I reached in and began tugging at Kalli's collar.

"A dog's mouth is far cleaner than a human mouth, believe me. Besides, we gave up on being germ-free a long time ago." She flashed me a brilliant smile. "No worries. It appears your baby and Tessa were both in need of a little diversion. That's an English cocker, isn't it?"

Thankfully, we were going to be spared giving another impromptu lecture.

I surrendered to the moment, smiling at the unfettered delight both young beings found in each other. Of course, the joy on Kalli's part was based on the tasty formula spread across the baby's face. She'd learned her lesson from Billy very well, indeed.

I scooped her in my arms and set her on the grass outside the van. "We really need to be going, but I'm so glad we didn't freak out your little girl."

Tessa's mom smiled. "Thanks for the fun."

Marc hooked the leash to Kalli's collar and we marched toward the frolicking dogs with purpose. Unfortunately, human goals didn't match the canine agenda. We were determined to give this group thing a solid try; Kalli was motivated to avoid it at all costs.

We deposited her next to a pug, who dropped a ball in front of her. Now if *that* wasn't an invitation to play. Kalli nudged the ball, and was still examining it when a chocolate Lab swept in, mouthed it, and took off for the far end of the field in a glorious example of canine efficiency. The pug took off after the large dog, clearly recognizing a soul mate.

Kalli yawned and flopped down.

"Perhaps we've had enough socializing for the time being," came Marc's carefully chosen words.

Later that evening, we reviewed the soccer field experience. While we acknowledged Kalli would never be a true team player, we concluded it was still a good idea to expose her to play groups, albeit in a limited way. When we did engage with other dogs, we learned to keep a close eye on her. We never knew where her boredom would lead her.

This lesson was reinforced when we joined a large group of dogs and their owners in a park by Lake Michigan one Saturday morning. We lost sight of Kalli in the heart of a dog cluster. When the animals dispersed, she had disappeared.

Trying to be calm, I said, "Marc? I must be blind. I don't see Kalli."

"Hmm. Me neither."

We wove our way among the dogs, searching for a little girl with black-and-white markings.

Nothing.

Panic had taken over at this point. I turned to Marc. "What could have happened to—" Why was he smiling?

He pointed in the distance, toward the parking lot.

There was Kalli, sprawled on the grass in front of our car. Waiting for us.

She emphasized her point by yawning and settling her head on her paws as she watched us approach. The perfect picture of blasé boredom.

You know I'm only humoring you guys by being here, right? If it were up to me, I'd be napping under that big tree in my backyard.

So, please don't push your luck. And don't expect me to be thrilled with this whole play group thing.

Hey, at least I'm being honest with you. There are dogs over there that would also love to be in the shade, snoozing away the afternoon, but they're such slaves to their humans they'd never dare to show the truth.

I don't think you guys appreciate how much dogs sacrifice for their people. At least you don't have to worry about that with me. I may be willing to work with you when it suits me, but I'm not sacrificing for anyone.

WHO'S TRAINING WHOM?

Mindful that our dog needed training along with socializing, Marc and I showed up for Kristen's beginning obedience class at a field house in one of Chicago's North Side parks.

Kalli came, too.

The parking lot filled quickly as the appointed hour approached. Car doors flung open and puppies popped out of vehicles with eager grins. Humans followed with apprehensive expressions. Marc and I joined the throng.

Kalli came, too.

She honored us by not screeching at her classmates. We considered that success and thought about leaving while we were ahead.

Marc shook his head. "Nope. We're staying. This will be fun. You'll see."

I looked back at him with eyebrows raised, trying to stay on my feet as Kalli lunged forward. "Heel" was going to be an interesting command for her.

Kristen encouraged us to sit on wooden benches strung along the walls of an auditorium in the field house. Puppies yipped and whimpered, testing the length of their leashes. Their owners exchanged confused smiles.

I glanced down at Kalli. The frenzy overtaking her was truly amazing. Crazed, hysterical, manic... The thesaurus couldn't come up with enough words to do her justice. At that moment, she was wiggling her way toward her neighbor—a three-month-old Rottweiler who was a tad larger than she was at six months. My eyes were riveted to giant paws. I could practically see the puppy growing before my eyes.

The Rottie's mom gave us a weary smile. "It's okay. Freddie's a lover. Never met a dog or human he didn't adore."

I let Kalli snuggle next to him. In turn, Freddie licked the top of her head. Then her sides and back. Then her legs. Within a few short minutes, her fur shone with slick slobber.

I stared at my dog in disbelief. I'd never known Kalli to warm up to any dog, yet here she was, a happy grin on her face as she settled next to the gentle, soon-to-be giant.

"I'm Weltha," Freddie's mom was saying. "And who are the parents of this cutie?"

Marc introduced us and launched into the English Cocker 101 speech that was already becoming a part of virtually every conversation we had when Kalli was around.

"She's adorable." Weltha reached down and tried to stroke her head.

Kalli ignored her.

A shiver of embarrassment coursed through me. This was the beginning of an unfortunate pattern I wasn't able to shake until Kalli was much older: considering my dog to be an extension of myself.

There were several troubling aspects to this reaction of mine. First, it failed to honor the fact that Kalli was very much her own unique entity who had a right to express herself as long as she wasn't hurting another living being. Second, it showed how incapable I was of accepting her honesty. Indeed, she was always very clear in her attitude toward others—human and animal alike. Some she greeted with pure joy. Others, like Weltha, she completely snubbed.

It took me years to understand that Kalli's unfettered response to others represented a valuable lesson-by-example for me. When I accepted that lesson, I became better at honoring my own gut-level assessment of people and situations, freeing me from the social conditioning of a childhood that had demanded I always "be nice and polite."

However, that first night of puppy obedience class found me way too nervous to entertain such reflections. And so, I mumbled an apology to Weltha and glared at Kalli.

She looked up at me with reproach in her eyes.

I know you like this lady, and I suspect you guys will become friends. But please don't expect me to feel the same way you do. I am my own dog, with my own opinions. And they don't have to make sense to you. Just respect them.

I forced my attention back to Weltha, asking about her animal and Kristen's class. I discovered the lady was a pro at obedience stuff. She and her husband had an older Rottweiler who had worked with Kristen in the past. They couldn't praise the trainer enough.

As for Freddie, he and Kalli were to become fast friends in the weeks ahead. The Rottweiler never lost his desire to give Kalli a bath with each class. And even though the puppy's tongue grew like a weed, along with the rest of him, Kalli didn't seem to mind. She accepted each bath as the appropriate way to end the evening.

My conversation with Freddie's mom was interrupted when Kristen strode to the center of the court, smiled, and launched into her opening speech. It was designed to encourage and support us. Yes, we can train these little buggers. Yes, the humans would learn as much as the dogs. Yes, any dog can be civilized.

Of course, we had to be diligent. Consistent. Dedicated. Responsible. Firm. Caring. Creative…

The check list went on. I had glazed over after "consistent," too distracted with the humming energy around me to pay close attention. I missed the cue for everyone to move to the center of the floor.

Marc nudged me. "Do you want me to take the first round?"

I shook my head. "I've got it." Kalli and I joined the group.

As we began learning how to "heel," little did I know she and I would spend many hours moving around a floor like this one, perfecting the basic commands, then the finer points of advanced obedience. However, at that moment, I had thoughts about nothing but trying to figure out a way to maintain some slack in the leash. This was no easy task since I had a rocket at the other end of the leather strip who was committed to propelling forward at warp speed. Dislocating my shoulder wasn't on my agenda for the evening.

Marc and I would soon discover that Kalli's steel-trap brain had no issues comprehending the commands. However, her high energy and insatiable fascination with new scents and sights threatened to sabotage everything we attempted to teach her.

Tracking instincts, bred deep in her bone, blossomed on the auditorium floor that evening. Marc and I spent much of our time trying to get her to focus on the task at hand. She ignored us, the slip-chain collar doing nothing to help us control her.

Frustration levels rose for man and beast alike. Finally, midpoint in the session, Kristen put us out of our misery. She approached with a metal object that appeared to be a torture device—a prong collar. Probably noticing what I'm sure was a horrified expression on my face, she smiled. "It's not as bad as it looks. Here, give me your wrist."

Obediently—humans followed Kristen's orders as readily as the dogs did—I extended my arm and wondered what was about to happen. She wrapped the thing around me and pulled it taut until the prongs pressed against my skin.

"Feel anything?" she queried.

"Nothing sharp or unpleasant. Just pressure." I turned to Marc and said, "Want to try it?"

"Nope." He winked at us. "I'll let you prove the point."

I rolled my eyes at Kristen.

She chuckled. "Anyway, you see that it doesn't hurt, right?"

I nodded.

"Willing to give it a try on Kalli?"

I looked down at the wriggling baby at my feet and nodded again.

A dramatic transformation unfolded before my eyes after the metal encircled Kalli's neck. Following Kristen's instructions, I gave the leash a quick jerk the next time Kalli surged on the "heel" command. Immediately, she settled against my leg.

Wide-eyed, I peeked at Marc, who was sitting on the bench across the room. He stared at us with his mouth open in shock. He gave me a halfhearted thumbs up.

Convinced this was too good to be true, I repeated the correction a few minutes later as Kalli picked up her pace and trotted ahead once again.

She slowed immediately.

Whoa! That thing really did get my attention. It doesn't hurt, but it feels...odd.

You understand you're cramping my style, right? 'Cause if you're going to keep using this neck thingie, I'm going to have to consider doing what you're asking.

Hmm... You may have won this round.

Thus began my love affair with the prong collar. Now, I realize many dog behaviorists deplore correction devices such as this one. A lovely philosophy of training that has achieved prominence since we started working with Kalli emphasizes positive reinforcement rather than discipline. And with stunning effect. But in that moment in Kristen's first class, the prong collar was a miracle.

(Note: We used the collar strictly for training purposes during those first classes and put it away the moment each class was over. Kalli was quick to learn that the device meant serious obedience work was at hand. This meant we rarely had to use the collar for correction after Kalli's initial exposure to it, and eventually we retired it altogether.)

Armed with an effective training tool, Marc and I drilled our dog in earnest. Our hard work with Kalli got us noticed in class a few weeks later. In the midst of an exercise in which the dogs were lined up across the room from their owners supposedly on a down-stay command, Kristen exploded in exasperation. More than half the animals had broken the directive and jumped up to visit with each other. She gestured toward Kalli, who had maintained her position on the floor, and yelled, "Everyone stop and look at that dog!"

The entire room froze.

"Kalli wants to get up more than anything. Do you have any idea how hard it is for her to hold that stay? But these people"—she pointed to Marc and me—"have taken the time to work with her at home until she learned to obey. Now, if they can do it with a hyper spaniel, certainly you guys can do it."

Okay, I object to being called hyper. I'd say "curious" is a better word.

But that aside, I knew I'd be admired for this. I pulled out all the stops, didn't I? And yeah, I really, really do want to sniff that corner over there. Especially after I saw that ugly black thing pee in it. But this game is so much more fun. I've managed to psych them out with my "good dog" routine. They're all so impressed. It's an easy audience.

Still...it's cool Mommy and Daddy are being recognized. They've been so good at following instructions. They deserve to be rewarded.

So, now that Kristen has made her point, should I get up and hit that corner? 'Cause I'm super bored right now. And above all things, I hate being bored!

But, no. I'd ruin everything. Better stay put.

Marc and I exchanged glances. What we thought would be a compliment had transformed into a comment we weren't sure how to interpret. However, it did spark serious motivation to keep working with our irascible dog. Because once you're noticed like that, you become a target for attention in every class that follows. Exactly what my overachiever self did not need.

We launched a dedicated training regimen I couldn't have imagined doing a few months before. Each morning, immediately after breakfast, I'd adorn Kalli with her prong collar and leash, and we'd hit the sidewalks of our neighborhood. She no longer screeched when she saw a non-spaniel, but as we'd discovered during Kristen's first class, Kalli's fascination with the world mixed with her natural tracking instinct, made her distraction-prone in the extreme. It threatened to derail obedience work at every turn.

The command, "heel," was a challenge from day one and continued to be for most of Kalli's life. Even with the prong collar, I struggled to settle her at my side. On her best days, she'd oblige me by trotting next to my leg for a half-block and then gradually slip ahead. If I wasn't paying close attention, I'd find her a dog's length in front of me. She'd toss me a withering look complete with raised eyebrows when I corrected her.

Hey, if you aren't going to focus, why should I?

After the collar correction, Kalli would settle back in place and begin the game all over again. And a game I'm sure it was, because while spaniels might be biddable, they are even more calculating.

So, last time we almost got to the end of the block before she realized I was walking ahead of her. I bet if I stay right by her side for the next block, she'll stop focusing on me so much and then I can screw around even more than I already have. You know, I may be onto something here. Let me analyze this for just a minute because I sense I'm close to brilliance.

I'm betting there's a formula to this. A half-block on command may well equal a full block off. And if I stay in position for...say, two blocks... Hmmm. I think I'll set up a test for this hypothesis.

Not to imply our training sessions were always such battles of will. Kalli was quick to learn the "down," "sit," and "stay" commands. And usually showed off her stuff whenever she was ordered to obey one or a combination of them. But streaks of independence were always just beneath the surface, waiting to reappear. And when they did, she was at her brilliant—and frustrating—best.

One beautiful fall morning, Kalli and I walked by the stretch of forest edging our neighborhood. A squirrel had been peeking out at us through bright red maple leaves from a heavy branch hanging over the sidewalk. Just as I commanded Kalli to "sit" and "stay," the squirrel dropped to the ground not more than ten feet from us.

Kalli's hunting instincts kicked into gear as the little animal made its move. Every doggie muscle tensed, her stub tail stuck straight out, rigid.

I wondered if she'd obey me.

She did. In her own way.

Very purposefully, she took two steps toward the squirrel and sat. She knew I was a newbie on the other end of the leash and waited to see what I'd do about this situation. She'd done what I'd asked of her...sort of. The extra two steps presented the dilemma for me.

Believe me, if someone had told me six months earlier I'd be concerned about those few inches, I would have assured them they were crazy. But that was before I'd begun working with Kristen. And she had made it clear humans were expected to toe a very careful line when interacting with dogs. That line was to be maintained. If the owner didn't hold firm, the pet would begin to take advantage.

In that moment, I knew I needed to make a point out of the fact that Kalli had fudged my order. Rather than repeat it—Kristen told us to utter the command only once—I checked Kalli's prong collar and uttered a firm, "No." And waited.

Without rising, she scooted her butt toward me a tinge. She had not placed herself in proper position, yet. But hey, I might accept this new spot. Who knew?

How's this? Close enough? You willing to buy it?

In for a penny, in for a pound. I gave her another correction.

She scooted back another fraction of an inch. Then looked at me with a huge grin on her face.

You gotta be willing to buy this. Right? This is good enough?

I started laughing. This dog knew exactly what she was supposed to do. And had decided to test me over it. And it wasn't a simple test. She was willing to be subtle, to carry the situation into a gray area of minute degrees. You have to respect an animal like that.

Through my laughter, I sputtered, "Kalli, give me a break. Just get back here."

And she did, adopting a perfect "heel" position even an AKC judge couldn't fault.

Kalli's unique approach to schooling her humans took many forms over the years we worked with her. A signature Kalli maneuver occurred one night during an advanced obedience session.

The exercise posed a deceptively simple challenge. The class formed a large circle in the middle of a gymnasium, dogs positioned at sit-stays by their handlers, who ordered them to hold the stay. The humans then moved to the opposite side of the circle. Everyone remained in place for several minutes...long enough for the less attentive pups to lose focus. Then Kristen cued the handlers to issue a recall command...in unison.

Within seconds, the still air in the cavernous room was shattered by twenty-five voices—including mine—calling to the dogs. Kalli obediently rose and began trotting toward me. Only to be mowed down by a slew of Labs dashing madly for their owners. She shook herself off and continued toward me, then executed a perfect "front and finish" around me. (This is a maneuver in which the dog arrives from a recall and sits directly in front of the handler. On cue, the dog moves to the left side of the human, turns in a counterclockwise half-circle, and sits close to the owner's left leg in "heel" position.)

The exercise was repeated. Again, Kalli set off toward me on cue. And was flattened by a scrambling Irish setter.

Third time revealed the true Kalli. As had been the case in the previous two instances, I called to her in unison with the others.

She didn't budge.

I broke the rules and called to her again, waving my arms furiously with the recall hand signal.

Nothing.

I couldn't believe she would so blatantly ignore my command. Growing angry, I watched her yawn while the other dogs rushed toward their humans.

When each was in its proper place by its owner, Kalli rose, the picture of nonchalance.

All eyes turned toward her.

She took in the attention and grinned. Yawned again. Gave herself a slow, leisurely shake, and ambled straight toward me.

Without waiting for my signal, she performed a textbook "front and by-heel" finish. (This maneuver involves the dog responding to the recall and sitting in front of the human, then walking around the handler's back until it's sitting next to the handler's left leg.)

That is what you wanted, isn't it?

What's that? You expected me to race into that madhouse with those lunatics again? Now who's the crazy one? And hey, it's not like I didn't obey you. But a dog has a right to protect herself.

I struggled with the moment. Part of me wanted to yell at her. The other part fell even deeper in love with her. The fact that she'd reasoned out the situation—and made a very intelligent decision as a result—wasn't lost on me. Did she follow the obedience playbook? Of course not. Did she use her head and play it smart? You bet.

We all started laughing. Except for Kristen. I could tell she was weighing the moment, trying to figure out how to respond. Finally, to her credit, she chuckled and bowed to my dog.

Kalli: one.

Humans: zero.

Kalli's score increased in the years ahead as her victories added up. Like the time Kristen's associate placed a huge tub of freeze-dried liver—the training treat of choice—in the middle of the gym floor and asked each of us to place our dog on one side of the tub and ourselves on the other. The challenge was to call in the dog, asking them to walk by the food without stopping.

I knew this was going to be a disaster the moment I saw the setup, but calmly waited in line with Kalli until it was our turn. I wondered why I was even bothering to go through the motions. Because there was no way my spaniel was going to leave those treats unmolested. Still, I plastered on my game face and prepared to start the exercise.

A look of supreme innocence spread across Kalli's face…except for the devilment dancing in her beautiful dark eyes. And she didn't disappoint. Her show-dog trot toward me in response to my grim "come" command was designed to be the consummate foil for the evil she planned. Kalli was nothing if not dramatic. If she could set up a situation for maximum impact, she would.

And she did.

Her rhythmic gait led her on a straight path to the tub. When she was within inches of it, she dropped to the floor in a classic sprawl, wrapped her front legs around the plastic container, and drew it close. Then, craning her neck ever so slightly, she snaked her muzzle over the tub's rim, dropped her mouth directly into the goodies, and began to eat. There was no hesitation on her part, no hint of shame in the face of her "disobedience," no obfuscation. Just the bliss that comes from crunching a beloved treat.

Hey, you can't expect me to do every little thing you tell me to. Remember I'm well known as a lover of fine food.

And a spaniel has her reputation to think of, after all. Now, leave me alone, I'm busy. Yuummmmmm.

Watching her, I shook off the mental image of a horse with a feedbag strapped to its face and acknowledged I had to go through the motions of correcting her and giving her another chance to get through the exercise successfully. Of course this was a supreme waste of time that only resulted in me admitting defeat in the face of her glorious style.

It was her nonchalance that turned this moment into a stellar example of Kalli in top form. She had identified a goal, formulated a plan, and implemented that plan with easy, perfect precision.

Another example of the spaniel at her best took place during the outdoor classes Kristen held at a lakefront park in Chicago. These sessions were always packed with students, their popularity revolving around the idyllic setting. Clear, azure skies, Lake Michigan waters gentling a mirror finish, and the bristling Chicago skyline made this the most amazing spot in the world to spend a Saturday morning in June.

Unless you were a spaniel who hated heat. Kalli tolerated this class by amusing herself with schemes, like playing tag with the trees when she was stuck in the sun. Her objective was simple: manage to just barely, kinda, right on the edge but who'll-notice-it's-so-close, obey the command-of-the-moment while maneuvering the human handler toward the closest patch of shade.

"Microscopic creeping" is what I called one version of this game. It was pure art in motion, and made her hustles during those first obedience walks through the neighborhood look like the unpolished work of the rookie she had been. However, that experience had nurtured the sophisticated animal who now confronted lakefront park challenges with style and panache.

Kalli launched microscopic creeping by stretching her body while holding a down-stay command. When done correctly, this could propel her forward at least a few inches. If she yawned while stretching, she netted a few inches more.

The key to Kalli's strategy came into play at this point. She capitalized on the fact that while I would notice her stretching, I'd dismiss it as nothing compromising the command. Thus, my guard was lowered, and my attention would shift elsewhere. This opened the door for her power move: a quick shuffle forward.

She repeated the entire process until she reached the shade.

Her natural élan now came into play as she celebrated success. Spaniel gloating was acceptable, if executed delicately. Too much threatened to expose the brilliant scheme, thus negating all achievement.

What course of action did she select? Feigning innocence.

You're checking up on me? Go right ahead. And while you're at it, just see how beautifully I've held this down-stay. Not a leg out of place.

Hmmm? You suspect I've moved just because you think I wasn't in the shade a minute ago and now I am? Oh, please. Did you see me move? I didn't think so. The heat must be getting to you. Remember, the sun travels in the sky so the shade is going to shift along with it. Didn't take that science class in school seriously, eh?

What's that? Okay, now you're getting tedious. Really, I've been in this very spot the whole time. Perhaps you backed up a few paces and you're the one out of position.

Hmmph! Humans!

I was determined to guide Kalli toward maturity as the ultimate trained, socialized dog who would be welcomed everywhere. Achieving this goal wasn't without its setbacks. Indeed, Kalli and I were kicked out of some of the very best places in Chicago as I resolutely introduced her to a variety of environments…some of which didn't welcome canines.

One classic ouster occurred during the heart of a rainy stretch of weather. The inclement conditions presented a real issue for me because Kalli was a puppy overflowing with nervous energy. If she didn't receive her daily ration of exercise and mental stimulation, energy escalated to frenzy. Besides which, I had a training regimen to honor.

At that time, I was focusing on distraction work. An efficient way to test whether an animal "gets" a lesson is to place it in the middle of a busy spot with strangers milling around, competing for its attention. If your dog can hold a down-stay on a crowded city sidewalk, you've achieved success.

As I watched the dreary showers fill yet another day, I realized Kalli and I had to leave the house and do something outside or we'd both go stir-crazy. My thoughts drifted to a nearby shopping center. It consisted of a huge complex of stores all strung together by a canopied pedestrian walkway. That canopy protected customers from the rain. It would protect a dog and her trainer from the elements, too. Best of all, those customers would provide Kalli's distraction.

The visit began as a trainer's dream. I heeled Kalli around shoppers, weaving her in and out. Down-stays occurred at out-of-the-way spots tucked by building corners so we wouldn't obstruct the flow of pedestrian traffic. I even managed a few recalls/fronts and finishes with her dragging the leash as she moved. All the while, rain drummed on the metal roof over our heads and not a drop landed on us.

Kalli and I were truly having fun. Of course, our fun took different forms. My version consisted of the satisfaction of seeing my dog perform her exercises flawlessly, even as people surged around her. Kalli's enjoyment derived from the idol worship she engendered in those people. Indeed, when you own an English cocker and you're out in the world with her, you have to accept that she's going to attract attention.

Besides which, it's my due. Those folks were showing excellent taste by adoring me. It was the least they could do. Look at how well I performed! Could any dog have done better?

Of course, I do require some dignity from people. That skinny lady with all the shopping bags really demeaned herself...oohing and aahing over me the way she did. I could barely maintain my down-stay. Geesh. Better she ignore me than ooze over me. Humans make fools out of themselves much too often, you know that?

Our idyllic afternoon was soon cut short when a rookie security guard arrived on the scene. I saw him out of the corner of my eye. He bristled with officious efficiency in his new uniform and shiny gun as he stalked toward us.

"Ma'am? Ma'am!"

I ignored him. After all, what could I have possibly done wrong? I continued my conversation with a charming elderly lady who had grown up with English cockers and thought Kalli was quite amazing.

"You can't be here with that...that...*dog*," he sputtered.

The senior citizen scowled at him.

I turned to face him with a smile. Gesturing at Kalli, who was in perfect heel position by my left ankle, I responded calmly, "Is there a problem?"

"Dogs are not allowed in the mall."

Uh oh. We're in trouble now. This guy is a real idiot. I'll be on my best behavior for sure. I don't want Momma to get into trouble.

"Mall?" I was genuinely confused. My arm swept toward the collection of free-standing stores that happened to have a metal roof over the sidewalk running between them. "What mall?"

Now he looked confused and started gesturing. "This mall. No dogs are allowed. It's in the rules." He fumbled in his pants pocket and pulled out a well-thumbed paperback manual. "Uh...Section 68, Paragraphs 34 through 36." Agitated fingers flipped pages.

"Oh, that's ridiculous," snapped the elderly woman.

"No kidding!" I turned at the sound of this new voice to see a small crowd had gathered behind us. The speaker was a young woman with a stroller brimming with twin toddlers. "I've been watching this dog. It's amazingly well trained." She smiled slightly. "Not to mention excellent entertainment for little ones on a rainy day."

A middle-aged businessman standing behind her spoke up. "That animal is better behaved than any of the kids you see running around here. If anyone should be banned, it's them!"

The storm had suddenly migrated to the security guard's face, spurred by defensive anger. He was being cornered by the crowd's disapproval, and he didn't like it. He had become a riled little man carrying a big gun.

I decided it was time to defuse the situation and plastered on my face what I hoped was a sweet smile in front of gritted teeth. "I understand you have rules to enforce. We'll be happy to go."

I turned toward the impromptu Kalli fan club and gave them a slight wave. Then, not being able to resist showing off my dog one last time, I gave her a quick flip of my hand—the signal for heel—and off we went toward the parking lot.

Kalli performed flawlessly on my left side. The rookie performed flawlessly on my right side—at least, according to Rule 84, Paragraph 6, Page 145. He accompanied us all the way to our car, huffing in self-importance with every arrogant step.

When we reached the car, I expected him to turn back and resume his mall duties. Instead, he stood by the front bumper, legs spread, hands on hips, a belligerent expression on his face. And didn't move a muscle as rain pelted him. Whereupon, Kalli and I settled in our nice, dry car and didn't budge. I figured he couldn't find a rule in his book that prohibited a person from having a dog in a private car in the parking lot. And I was sufficiently incensed to make a point of it.

He faced my sweeping windshield wipers, staring at us, raindrops dripping from the visor of his cap and onto the tip of his nose.

I stared back.

He broke eye contact with me, shifting from foot to foot, his discomfort obvious.

I continued staring.

With a final huff, he turned on his heels and stalked toward the shopping complex, his back as stiff as if he had a ramrod stuffed under his clothes.

Kalli nudged my arm with her muzzle.

Good one, Mom. You really showed him. But for now, let him go. He's one unhappy person. Bet he doesn't even have a dog, although he certainly needs one. We should feel sorry for him.

CANINE GOOD CITIZEN

Our obedience classes and training drills led Kalli, Marc, and me to our first official hurdle: the Canine Good Citizen test. Created by the AKC in the 1980s, the ten-step examination is designed to motivate humans to mold a dog into a civilized being, especially in public. It focuses on acknowledging good manners with a certificate awarded to those passing it and the right to slap a "CGC" after the name of the pet.

In order to earn this honor, the animal must be willing to be groomed and handled without complaint, greet a stranger calmly, walk on a leash without pulling, move through a crowd of people with ease, and perform basic obedience maneuvers. Other behavioral aspects include the pet's ability to be around other humans with dogs without freaking out, and handle distractions such as sudden noises and a wheelchair rolling nearby. Finally, the handler is required to leave the dog alone on a fifteen-foot tie-out, checking to make certain it's well-adjusted enough to accept this situation without fuss.

Nothing involved in this exam was new to us. We'd socialized Kalli to the point where she'd interacted with folks in wheelchairs and on crutches, and was comfortable with humans accompanied by dogs. She was groomed monthly. And the little girl knew her commands. A sudden loud noise in her vicinity? No problem. She was equally unflappable when left alone tied to a lamp post in front of a store. The real question was, would she be willing to show off these abilities when we asked her to?

The day of the test found me uncharacteristically casual. I've never been terribly interested in the standards issued by the AKC. Their obedience trials and the hoops one has to jump through to accumulate points toward a title never seemed important to me. Then again, I'm not earning a living as a breeder, handler, or trainer.

However, my personal goals for Kalli and me—based on the demands of the wacky, value-ridden, perfectionist slave driver residing inside my head—soon got the better of me, setting my nerves ablaze. And so it was that my "whatever" mood disappeared as I led Kalli to the center of the gymnasium that evening. Suddenly, I wanted those stupid letters after her name very much.

Kalli ignored my change in attitude. She was her normal, happy self…butt a blur as she greeted each human and dog within eyeshot.

When her nose hit the floor, my warning system kicked in. I studied her carefully, trying to gauge her distraction level on a scale of one to ten. If those smells she was sucking up her nostrils were really compelling, she might be peaking near ten, in which case we didn't stand a chance of obtaining the certificate. If the smells and sights weren't that unusual, the scale would settle at five or six, and I could be hopeful about the evening's outcome…as long as I established my alpha dominance from the outset. (Okay, so I never did achieve alpha status with her, but she was kind enough to let me think I had.)

The exam began and we stepped out, Kalli heeling by my side. The activity didn't have to be perfect, only implemented such that the dog wasn't pulling a tight leash. Kalli started to forge ahead as we approached Kristen. I decided I wasn't going to put up with any nonsense, but to do that, I had to get her attention immediately.

"Back!" I snarled.

She slowed her pace.

Wow. We might actually make it through this.

At the trainer's side now, I ordered Kalli to sit. She did.

Okay.

Kristen reached down with a grooming brush and began stroking her back. Kalli's stub tail revved to hyper mode. Bystanders giggled.

Knowing she was a crowd favorite, Kalli yipped with a big smile on her face.

Hey, the crowd loves me. My people!

...Hmmm? What's that? You want me to do what now? I don't want to walk over to that lady and her ugly mutt. I want to stay with Kristen! She has freeze-dried liver in her pocket.

...Hmmm? Are you going to make a big deal out of this? You are?

Well, where's your food?

No food? You've got to be kidding me.

Oh, geesh. You sound really serious.

Okaaaaay. I'm moving.

Kalli was slow to respond as I edged her over to a volunteer—a friendly stranger with a black Lab the size of a bear by her side. The trick was to get Kalli to sit and hold her position next to me while the other human and I shook hands. To do this successfully, Kalli had to ignore the other dog. Any overt attempt on her part to interact with it and we failed the exercise.

I figured my chances to maintain control would improve with maximum space between her and the Lab, so I began gauging our distance from the pair as we approached them. Then I assessed the length of the woman's right arm with a critical eye. These measurements were crucial as I calculated exactly how far away from her I could stop and seat Kalli, and still be able to physically reach her hand. No artisan ever created a masterpiece with more careful measurements than my assessment of that gym floor. With great precision, I picked my spot, reached it, and ordered Kalli to "sit" and "stay."

Not a problem. The butt dropped on cue. But it was wiggling furiously as her enthusiasm for the moment grew. A bad sign. Additional indicators didn't encourage me, either. The other animal whined and fussed, obviously desperate to reach Kalli.

Now we were on the edge of a precipice. Kalli's butt still maintained contact with the floor, but I could feel her weight starting to shift to her front legs. The little bugger was preparing to get up.

So I have a big decision to make. Do I tease that stupid black thing? This is soooo tempting because I'm betting it has the brain of a pea. Just think of all the fun I could have tormenting it.

But that would upset Mommy.

Besides, now that I think about it, hustling that dog would be way too easy. If there's no challenge, where's the fun? And hey, if I forgo this opportunity and listen to Mommy, I'd be helping her out. After all, this dumb activity is a big deal to her. She'd be so pleased with me if I was good.

I bet she'd give me extra treats.

What to do? What to do?

And then the unimaginable happened. Kalli settled back down.

By now, my fingers had actually made physical contact with the other person's. Soon, we were shaking hands. Kalli remained seated. I can't say as much for the Lab. The black giant rose on all four paws and started careening toward us.

Inwardly, I groaned. That other dog was going to ruin the test for us. Or was it? Kalli hadn't moved, and the handshaking portion of the exam was over. I heard Kristen's urgent voice behind me. "That's good, Laura. You and Kalli can move on."

I heeled Kalli out of there as fast as I could.

After that close call, the rest of the test was a piece of cake. By the end of the evening, we'd earned the right to have the letters, "CGC," follow Kalli's name for the rest of her life.

Brimming with pride as we drove home that evening, I stole a glance at Kalli in the back seat as I waited for a traffic light to turn green. Even sound asleep, my dog's smugness radiated from every pore of her body. Situation normal.

SOCIAL BUTTERFLY

Marc and I balanced Kalli's obedience work with activities designed to encourage her socializing with our neighborhood dog group...like their Halloween party. I immediately got caught up in the group's enthusiasm for the event, which seemed to revolve around doggie costumes.

"It's great fun," oozed Ellen as she draped a hand over her Irish setter. "Last year, I dressed up Artie as a pirate, complete with eye patch." I glanced at the large sporting dog, who returned my gaze with a goofy smile. Yup. I could see that.

"We had tons of great costumes in the group," Ellen went on. "Everything from Darth Vadars and skeletons, to doggie dinosaurs and piglets."

"Piglets?" Marc raised an eyebrow.

"Oh, for the little ones," Ellen quickly answered. "Pugs and one Chihuahua."

"I don't know that Kalli would go for something like that." Marc gave me a penetrating look that meant, "Go slow, kid. This doesn't feel right."

I ignored him. "That does sound like fun." I looked down at Kalli, who was sitting by my side, yawning. She'd had her fill of the group for the day.

"Oh, I can just see your dog all dressed up," enthused Ellen. "Like a cheerleader or a fairy, perhaps. She's such a perfect doll. You could put her in anything and she'd be queen of the ball." She paused, then said, "I know! Scarlett O'Hara! Can't you imagine her in a hoop skirt, sprawled on the lawn at Tara?"

I began to understand Marc's skepticism. "Um. Maybe."

That evening, Marc eyed me over the top of his scotch as we relaxed in the living room. "You're not really serious about sticking Kalli in a costume, are you?"

"I am, actually." I inwardly winced at my defensive tone. "I think it might be great fun."

"For whom? Kalli? Or you?"

A brilliant question, Daddy. I'd kinda like to know that, too.

Really, Mommy, you aren't going to do this to me, are you? I mean, I'm just not that kind of dog to do the costume thing. All this time, I've humored you by going to that stupid group. I knew it was important to you, and I wanted to cooperate. But there are times when all self-respecting dogs have to draw the line. And this is one of those times.

A piggie? Scarlett O'Hara? What are you thinking?

Hmmmm. If I pretend this is all a bad dream and go on as if nothing is happening, perhaps I can convince you to do that, too.

That's right! That's the ticket. The power of my spaniel brain will take over and mind-meld with you, and you'll forget all about this.

Forget all about this.

Forget...forget...

Marc and I forged ahead with our plan to find Kalli a costume. Well, I forged ahead and Marc humored me. Kalli ignored the whole affair.

I dragged Marc to three PetSmart stores on the weekend before Halloween. At each one, we rummaged through the racks of picked-over costumes and found nothing "suitable." On to human stores.

Marc shook his head as we parked outside a local Target. "Are you sure about this?" He turned to face me from the driver's seat of our

SUV. "Maybe the fact that we can't find a costume for Kalli is an…omen…or something."

I couldn't help but laugh at his silly reasoning. "Come on, Alpha Dad. This will be fun."

"Right," he grumbled as we got out of the car.

I led him into the children's department. It appeared that puppy Kalli could wear a human toddler's size, 2T. And the search for a perfect costume was on.

"Okay, this can't get any sillier." Marc held up a fairy costume, complete with golden-toned leotard and a stiff tutu.

I couldn't have agreed more. We caught each other's eye and burst into laughter.

I sputtered, "I think that might restrict her movement just a tad, don't you?" Marc wiped tears from his eyes and returned the fairy to her rightful place on the rack.

"We could turn her into a little witch." I grabbed a black onesie, complete with teeny cone hat.

"You thought the fairy was restrictive?" As soon as the words were out of his mouth, Marc started laughing again. Soon we were both howling, struck with the absurdity of the situation.

"A restrictive fairy!" I sputtered. We broke out in fresh gales of laughter.

By this time, we were beginning to attract disapproving attention from other customers in the store. Drying our eyes, we toned down our outbursts to chuckles and continued pawing through the rack.

Finally, I found a cow costume that begged me to pull it out of the bunch. It was lightweight, with Velcro straps. Perky pink ears topped the ensemble.

Marc agreed that it would be comfortable for Kalli to wear, and it would transform her into the perfectly attired Halloween spaniel. It was a done deal.

Perhaps we should have reconsidered.

At least Kalli didn't bite off our hands as we fit the thing to her body. Indeed, the cotton costume fit her to a tee.

"You know, I'd say she's actually proud of herself in that thing," Marc murmured as we watched her prance around the kitchen.

Proud? Are you out of your mind??? But I have realized that I have no choice in this stupid affair. I've decided to be graceful in the moment.

I will tell you one thing, though. I will never, ever wear another costume, nor any miscellaneous parts of a costume, ever again. Once is quite enough.

So while I will go to your stupid party and play the fool because that is what you want me to do, this will not happen again.

Oh, I know you don't realize the long-term effects of today's actions, but you will rue the day you put me through this.

Now that I've made myself perfectly clear, would you please straighten these stupid ears? There's nothing sillier than crooked cow ears.

Suddenly, I noticed the costume ears were listing to one side. As I reached down to adjust them, I stifled my giggles, knowing that Kalli hated to be laughed at. I stood back and watched Kalli sniff around the kitchen floor, à la cow, black spots and all.

Black spots...

"Um, you notice anything about Kalli's current appearance when you compare it to our dog *sans* costume?" I didn't dare look at Marc as I said this.

"What do you mean?"

I spoke carefully, trying not to laugh. "Well, we have a black-and-white dog in a black-and-white costume." The last word disappeared in a sputter I couldn't tamp down.

"Oh, my God. This is too funny."

To Kalli's credit, she played her cow role at the party with dignity and style. I suspected she was furious beneath her calm exterior.

I noticed her staring at the other dogs at the party and I could see why. Some of the costumes were amazingly…er… Okay, I'll admit it. They were stupid. Golden retrievers masqueraded as giant bumble bees, bulldogs dressed up as convicts (also in black and white), Chihuahuas appeared as hot dogs. We watched a Jack Russell terrier racing around as Superman, a yellow Lab as Batman, and an American cocker spaniel imitating a policeman.

I sighed and looked down at my dog. "This is what you were trying to tell me, wasn't it? This whole costume thing is just not for the likes of a dignified spaniel like you."

I could have sworn I saw a look of triumph cross Kalli's eyes before she wandered off to investigate a stretch of low ground in one corner of the soccer field. It was Kalli's favorite spot because it was always damp and teemed with wonderful smells. Turning around, I saw a look of horror pass over Marc's face.

"What?"

"Check her out," he said in grim tones.

I glanced over my shoulder in time to see Kalli trotting back to us with a satisfied look on her face and a jauntiness in her step. Mud covered her from head to toe. Her formerly brilliant black-and-white costume was now a dripping uniform shade of dark brown. Kalli had been transformed into Swamp Thing. Who needed a Target costume when nature provided the camouflage for free?

She dropped in front of us, and I watched her smile widen into a mud-eating grin. Literally.

"Well, I guess she told us," Marc grumbled in my ear. He hated to see her dirty and complained each time we had to clean her up. This mud-swathed version of his dog had not made him a happy camper.

I nodded, carefully not looking at him as I returned Kalli's grin. I'd received her message and couldn't help but admire the clarity with which she had communicated it. Her calmness in the face of the cow transformation had been a façade. Underneath it, she'd executed her revenge to perfection. Since the weather had been rainy for days before the party, she knew the low spot in the field would be muddy. What a perfect place to undergo a spaniel metamorphosis. She'd managed to turn the events around to suit her purposes.

Kalli style.

Halloween wasn't the only holiday celebrated by the neighborhood doggie play group. It turned out that Christmas also demanded an event—a trip to the local PetSmart to visit Santa.

"I promise there will be no costumes involved," I assured Kalli as I rummaged through the holiday collars at our corner pet store. "Except for maybe a decorative collar like this one." I held up a strip of red velvet with green mistletoe embroidery around the clasp.

Kalli sniffed it and huffed.

"Oh, come on. You can't possibly take offense at this. It's positively…elegant." I wrapped it around my wrist. "See? I could wear it as a bracelet."

Be my guest. And while we're on the topic, why is it that I'm forced to wear something weird every time we do one of these special occasion things with that stupid group?

Hmmmm? I know it would mean a great deal to you if I wore the collar. Oh, geesh. Now you're trying to make me feel guilty.

Alriiiiiight. I guess the thing isn't that ugly. At least the red provides a pleasant contrast to my blue roan coloring. I'll wear it, already.

On the appointed day of our PetSmart field trip, I fastened the festive collar around Kalli's neck with satisfaction. She was adorable, whether she wanted to be or not. Marc insisted upon snapping a few photos and then we were off to let a professional take the next pictures with Santa. Our hopes were high. We were just sure the outing would yield the perfect Kalli snapshot for our Christmas cards that year.

Customers—human and dog—packed the store. We could barely squeeze through the doors to enter the space. Excitement and holiday cheer rippled through the crowd, punctuated by laughter as folks pointed to dogs bedecked as Santas, elves, and reindeers.

Kalli was decidedly underdressed.

"I hope you're happy," I said to her, pointing to a German shorthaired pointer exquisitely attired as Mrs. Claus. "You're one of the few dogs in here without a costume."

Kalli had been inhaling the smells in every inch of the store. She broke off her exploration to look at me with one raised eyebrow.

"She's perfectly attired," Marc scolded me gently. "By far the most elegant dog here."

"No doubt," I muttered. "So, where is our group?"

"I think I see Artie over there dressed up like a reindeer." Marc pointed vaguely toward the back of the store as he referred to Ellen's Irish setter. "Yup, that's him. I just saw Ellen try to haul him over to her side."

I chuckled as I gathered the leash and led Kalli through the crowd. Artie had never learned manners. Given the size and weight of the massive mahogany dog, he gave Ellen a real run for her money when she needed to keep him under control.

"Oh, by God, she's adoooooorable," trilled Ellen, her eyes glued on Kalli as we approached. "Where did you find that scrumptious collar?"

"It's nothing compared to Artie." I pointed to the reindeer costume. "He looks like he's ready to pull Santa's sleigh."

"He'd be happier pulling the sleigh than hanging out here, that's for sure." Ellen laughed. "Artie isn't crazy about crowds pressing in on him."

I nodded, noting the setter's panting and crazed expression. "Well, it'll be over soon enough."

"I doubt it. Did you take a look at the line to see Santa?" Ellen gestured over her shoulder.

"Oh, brother." I eyed a string of humans and dogs stretching the entire length of the store. The throng I'd identified as a crowd actually *was* the line.

"Any idea how long this is going to take?" Marc asked our doggie group aficionado.

Ellen shook her head. "By the looks of that Santa, I'd say we're going to be here a while."

I jockeyed around a few folks to get a view of a hulking, throne-like chair draped in fake holly. Precariously perched on a massive, red velvet cushion sat a child—all right, he probably was a teenager, but he looked like a little kid to me—drowning in the velour of an oversized Santa costume. His beard seemed to be choking him as his tiny button mouth spit out continuous puffs of white fuzz. Blinking eyes barely cleared the white cottony stuff. They widened in panic as a rambunctious Irish wolfhound, dressed like an elf, half-climbed on his lap and started licking the fake facial hair. The hound's pointy elf ears stabbed the air with each lick.

The teen shrank into his Santa garb, pressing against the towering red throne as he tried to create as much distance as possible from the crazed canine elf. The Santa velour swallowed more and more of him until the only things visible were two bug eyes and flailing fingers peeking out from dripping red sleeves.

A second teenager stood behind a camera that was set on a tripod a few feet from the throne. He occupied himself snapping gum and yawning between pictures. Over the teenager's shoulder, an elderly woman trilled to the wolfhound, "Binky, darling, sit. Stay. That's a good girl. Noooooo. I said, sit. Sit, Binky. Binky? Did you hear me?"

"How could Binky not hear her with that voice?" drawled Marc in my ear. "If it gets much shriller, it'll break glass."

I giggled. "That dog has long since stopped listening to her."

"Smart dog."

As Binky's owner continued to barrage the dog with commands, we dutifully took our place at the end of the line. I glanced down as Kalli tugged on the leash. She was maneuvering so she could investigate the smells coming from a nearby display stuffed with Christmas rawhide chews. I let out the leash a bit so she could get closer to the exotic odors.

As long as she was happy, I was happy.

The line inched forward.

Soon, Kalli had run out of smells within the limited range of the leash. She plopped down in front of me, glaring into my eyes.

Look, if I'm going to suffer through this silliness, the least you can do is entertain me. I mean, I've been gracious...ignoring the kids stepping on my paws, allowing strange humans to pet me. I haven't even pottied on the floor, although I really have to go.

Speaking of which, I am now officially changing my look to one imploring you to take me outside. Ready? Here comes the change. Don't miss it.

Theeeeeere.

Mom? Look into my eyes, Mom. Ah, yes. I can see recognition dawning. Indeed, your sweetie would like to go OUTSIDE.

Marc had been watching the silent exchange between us and picked up Kalli's silent plea at the same time I did. "Go ahead and take her out. I'll hold the place in line."

We strolled around the building until we reached a strip of lawn. It was packed with humans walking their dogs, each muttering encouraging words about going potty, and piddling, and going poo poo, and so forth.

Without seeing her face, I knew Kalli was eyeing this scene with one of her famous eyebrow-raised looks of distain. "I know," I told her. "You think they're idiots and we need to find some other place for you."

I glanced around me. The brilliant, sun-filled afternoon had turned dour and cloudy. The temperature had dropped at least ten degrees since we'd arrived at the store, and the wind coming off the lake had picked up. Sheets of cold air wrapped around us like a numbing shroud. But Kalli seemed oblivious to the inclement weather. Sensing new territory to explore, she pulled me toward a field behind the store.

Eyeing the choppy, ice-encrusted landscape, I shook my head and stifled a sigh. Owning a sporting dog meant spending long minutes in such places. Glad I'd worn heavy boots with thick treads, I plunged into the field with Kalli, letting her off leash as soon as we had distanced ourselves from the loading dock that stretched across the back of the building.

Kalli took off at a run, then stopped abruptly midway across the field. Immediately, squawking reverberated in the frozen trenches as a quail appeared and flapped furiously into the air. I'm sure the bird was flinging evil epithets at my dog. But Kalli seemed to take the insults in stride as she turned around and trotted back to me with a triumphant grin spread across her muzzle. The flusher/retriever had done her job.

"Um. Didn't you forget something?" I asked her.

On cue, Kalli executed an about-face and squatted in front of a heap of frosty weeds. Then she trotted into the heart of the field at a leisurely pace. Thus began a mental exercise on my part, well known to most dog owners. How long was I willing to stand there and let her wander? Certainly, the Santa line wasn't rushing us, so I could legitimately let her stay outside for a while. But I was bored and cold, and not inclined to let her linger in the frigid air. Besides, we'd already had our walk for the day.

I called her to me. Her head popped up, and she gave me a surprised look.

"Yeah, I know. I usually stand around waiting for you, but not today."

She continued to stare.

"Do you need a formal command? Come on, Kalli. Seriously, I'm not standing here any longer."

Grudging acceptance weighed down her every step as Kalli wove her way back to me. She gave wide berth to every frozen clump of weeds as her serpentine pattern propelled her from one side of the field to the other.

Kalli choreographed her casual recall with consummate perfection, meandering just enough to communicate her displeasure that I was cutting short her fun, but direct enough so she didn't appear to be ignoring me.

Finally sitting in front of me, she gave me a big grin.

Ah! Guess I told you, didn't I? Now then, what's next? Oh, that's right. I get to follow in Binky's giant paw prints and get my picture taken with Santa.

Yaaaaawn. Well? Let's get it over with.

Snapping the leash onto Kalli's collar, I acknowledged, yet again, she might be frustrating, but she was never boring.

Upon our return to the stuffy, overcrowded store, I discovered Marc had moved up in line much faster than I had thought he would. We were now only one human-and-dog combo away from Santa.

I looked off to one side and saw Ellen popping a treat in Artie's mouth. She grasped a photo in the other hand. In response to my questioning gaze, she mouthed, "Wonderful!"

Nodding, I smiled at her exuberance and wondered what Artie's picture really looked like.

The pair in front of us—a human and his chocolate Lab dressed as a court jester, complete with bells and pointy hat—reached Santa. The junior photographer had just finished placing the dog by Santa's side, when the Lab's owner stormed up the steps to the throne, yelling, "No, no, no. That's Hershey's bad side. His profile is quite unsuitable for a picture. He has to be positioned differently."

Evidently, Hershey's owner wanted the PetSmart picture to be studio quality.

Santa's helper stared at the man for several long seconds, gum popping. Then he mumbled, "We can't do that, sir."

"What? What? That's preposterous. I'm paying for this photograph. I want it right!"

The teenager shrugged. "We were told that every dog has to be in the same place by Santa."

The man tsked his impatience, then turned to his dog. "Hershey, come!"

The Lab executed a perfect front and finish before his human.

I happened to glance down at Kalli, who was stirring restlessly at my feet. She seemed to sense my gaze and looked up at me. I could see my disgust reflected in her expression. "I know," I said to her softly. "There's one in every crowd, isn't there?"

I could have sworn she rolled her eyes at me in agreement.

Hershey's human waved an authoritarian finger through the air. The Lab followed the gesture with precision, trotting to Santa's side.

After another hand signal, the Lab dropped to the floor at the teenager's feet, looking positively regal. This was quite an accomplishment considering that his pointy hat jingled and bobbed with his every move and was now slipping over one eye.

"You…you…can't let your dog lie there," Santa said. "We'll get into trouble."

"Nonsense," replied Hershey's human. "This is eminently better suited for the occasion." He whirled around to face us, arms extended as if he were a conductor and we were all instruments in his orchestra. "Don't you all agree?" he said to us. Then, with a patronizing smile pasted on his face, he drifted down the steps from the platform. "*Now* you may take your picture," he thundered in sonorous tones over his shoulder.

The teen cowered behind the camera, clearly as much at a loss in the situation as Santa was. He swayed back and forth, hands waving around the camera in a helpless gesture.

Santa persisted. "Sir, we have rules we have to follow."

"Take the picture," Hershey's human commanded.

With shaking fingers, the teen began to snap the photographs. Hershey, who seemed accustomed to having his picture taken, preened before the lens. His grin expressed all the delight and bonhomie lacking in his human. Nature's own balancing act, I mused.

I glanced down to see Kalli eyeing the scene intently.

"If I didn't know better, I'd swear she's chuckling," Marc whispered in my ear. I nodded, grateful that she was quiet and composed.

"Let's go," Marc said.

I looked up to see the Lab jester and human duo exit stage left. The man had cornered a hapless young female employee, waving the photo in her face. I noticed the girl had the same blank expression on her face that Santa had adopted. Shaking my head, I guided Kalli toward the throne.

Kalli paused and looked back at me, a question in her eyes. I knew exactly what she was asking. She wanted permission to play the situation with the teenagers as she saw fit, free from my intervention and commands. My instincts overrode my dog trainer role. I nodded slightly, dropped the leash, and watched the show.

Kalli fixed Santa with her clear brown eyes and set her butt in motion. When the child saw her wriggling body and unmistakably friendly overtures, he smiled.

She reached him and stood quietly by his leg. He held out a hand to her, and Kalli licked it. Watching him react to Kalli was like observing a tight spring unwinding.

"She's really cute," came muffled words behind the white fluff.

Kalli adopted a play bow and woofed softly at him.

If you don't relax, you're going to make yourself sick. I mean, you're stuck here for the rest of the day, so why not have some fun?

Hmmmm? Yeah, I know this is not what you were expecting when you showed up for work this morning. Some of the dogs have been real pills, haven't they? Like that Dinky or Rinky or Blinky or whatever that stupid dog was named. Not to mention the idiot humans like Hershey's dad. But you're with Mom and Dad and me, now. So, let's play a bit.

See? I'm wiggling my butt in the very cutest way I can. And look at this gorgeous collar Mom put on me. I'm even more adorable than I usually am.

Okay. Much better. You're actually starting to enjoy yourself, I can tell. So, let's get this photo taken while we're all in a good mood.

Here I go...sitting exactly where you want me to for this stupid picture thing. You won't get into any trouble with me controlling things. I'm even going to smile.

Cheeeeese!

I couldn't have been more proud of Kalli. She posed perfectly for the camera, right on the designated spot. The smile on her face was a delight to behold.

I heard voices behind me as I watched her, entranced.

"Isn't she the most adorable thing you've ever seen?"

"I wonder what kind of dog she is?"

"Such a perfect size. And so well-mannered."

As for the resulting photos… Well, let's just say I was grateful Marc had snapped a few pictures before the outing.

ALL WORK AND NO PLAY

It took me a while to figure out that while obedience classes and afternoons with our neighborhood doggie play group were excellent ways for Kalli to spend time and blow off energy, she needed to have some fun, too…on her own terms. I purchased a long leash and we were ready to party.

On a beautiful October afternoon, I loaded Kalli into the car and we headed to the lakefront of southeast Evanston. Kalli's nose was in hyper-drive the minute she hit the ground of a beautiful park running along Lake Michigan. Soon, we were ambling among towering oak trees sporting brilliant orange leaves. Crisp air drifted over sparkling blue water as we approached a stretch of pristine beach.

I noticed an older lady approaching us, a leash in one hand. It was the harnessed beast at the other end of the leather strip that attracted our attention. Bobbing along in perfect heel position was a ferret.

The woman turned off the path before she reached us and led the diminutive creature onto an expanse of sand bordering the water. Letting the ferret off leash, she stood back and chuckled. When we drew nearer, I saw the little guy was hard at work building an elaborate network of tunnels in the sand.

By this point, Kalli was pulling at the leash, trying to get to the ferret. I reined her in and kept her close by my side, not wanting to interfere with the construction project.

The ferret's owner looked up and grinned. "D'Artagnan does this every time we come to the park."

D'Artagnan?

"He thinks the beach is his own personal sandbox," she continued.

I returned her smile. "He's amazing. I've never seen anything like him."

"Oh, honey. This is normal ferret behavior." Just then, the little guy's head popped up through the sand and he threw us a big smile. At least, I think it was a smile.

"What a cute dog! If you want to let her off leash to play with D'Artagnan, that would be fine with us. He loves dogs."

My mind processed the possibilities at warp speed. None of them were positive. After all, Kalli was bred to be a hunter and her instincts were strong. And while spaniels usually focus on game birds in the field—indeed, the word "cocker" is derived from the breed's principal target in England, the gamecock—I couldn't be certain their list of prey didn't include small rodents.

"Oh, I don't know..." I hedged.

She placed a hand on my arm, her clear blue eyes sparkling. "Trust me, they'll be fine together."

"But she's a sporting dog."

D'Artagnan's owner shook her head, the picture of calm certainty. "I know whereof I speak. Let them have a chance to play together."

Her words resonated with me. Once I'd acknowledged how restrictive I'd been with Kalli, I realized I needed to lighten up. D'Artagnan and his owner were offering me an opportunity to do just that. Shrugging, I unleashed my hound.

I suspect Kalli hadn't thought there was a chance in hell she'd be allowed to meet the ferret. The sudden release of her restraints took her by complete surprise. She lurched forward in her newfound freedom, almost landing on her nose.

She flashed me a confused look.

Wow. You're actually letting me off leash? To play? Really? With that little beastie thing? What did you do with my mom?

Okay, well, before you change your mind...

And she was off in a mad dash down the beach, paws flying in all directions, long ears flapping in the crisp fall breeze.

The ferret had popped up through a hole in one of his tunnels and watched Kalli scramble toward him. As she drew near, he leaped in the air with an excited squeak and dove into the hole just as she reached him.

She skidded to a stop, sand spraying under her paws, tail wagging furiously. D'Artagnan appeared at the hole, then popped out of sight once again. She dropped into a play bow and woofed at the ferret for emphasis, completely focused on the spot where she'd last seen him.

D'Artagnan had wriggled his way down one impromptu tunnel to a spot off to Kalli's side. He squeaked again in this new location, and she whirled toward him. He scampered down the tunnel. Kalli was on his heels, flattening the sand behind him.

The game was afoot...literally. Kalli's paws splayed across each leg of the tunnel as she chased D'Artagnan. When she caught up to him, I held my breath. No more than a few inches separated the two creatures. Then they touched noses.

I needn't have worried. Kalli was smitten with the little guy. A grooming session began, and D'Artagnan basked under the warm moisture of her tongue.

Chuckling behind me attracted my attention, and I turned to see a group had formed around us. Joggers, strollers, and other dog-walkers had stopped to watch the antics of the spaniel and the ferret. A wave of laughter drew my focus back to my dog, who was now chasing the little guy among the sandy mounds. The lightning-fast D'Artagnan had a definite advantage and was out-maneuvering Kalli easily. But he appeared to deliberately slow down just enough to allow her to draw near before he streaked away from her once again.

Kalli took the game in stride, legs and paws flailing, tongue lolling out one side of her mouth, eyes wild with glee. I couldn't have asked for a better exercise session.

It took the two critters long minutes before they tired. Finally, though, the pair flopped on the sand in peaceful accord.

Kalli found other curious playmates on the beaches of Evanston in the months and years ahead. One afternoon, she and I rounded a curve of the shoreline to find a flock of barn swallows frolicking in the gentle breeze as they swooped over the sand and water. Kalli froze in place, mesmerized by the sight.

Knowing she had no chance to catch or harm the birds, I let her off leash to play with them. And play they did. These graceful birds knew exactly how low to swoop over her head to remain safe and still tease her into chasing them. Their lyrical chirps filled the air as they careened overhead, then skimmed the surface of the beach in a clear invitation for Kalli to play tag with them. She gave as good as she got, spinning and circling in their wake, stalking those that landed.

They even taught Kalli to swim. She'd padded through the water before, of course, but had only waded near the beach. Under the bewitching influence of the swallows, she drifted farther and farther away from shoreline as she followed the gentle curve of wings swirling around her head. Her legs began to stroke through the water with an even, gliding motion. She'd left terra firma and was embracing the water.

Captured by the joy of the moment, it took me a while to realize my dog was paddling away. Which wouldn't have been a problem except I don't swim and I wasn't sure I could get her back.

I glanced around for human assistance, should I need it, and tried to control my rising panic. The deserted beach offered no help. And Kalli was disappearing from view, the top of her head merely a speck on the horizon.

If there was ever a time for a successful recall, this was it.

I called out to her, attempting to edit the wavery fear from my voice. "Kalli! Come!" I held my breath, stuffing down the nasty stabs of anxiety taunting me with the possibility she'd completely ignore me.

The speck disappeared.

Swearing at myself for never having learned to swim, I kicked off my shoes, preparing to jump in and go after her. With unswerving certainty, I knew that I *would* save my dog, even at the risk of my own life.

I took one more frantic look. Nothing. Just gently rolling waves.

I stepped into the lake and began wading out into the endless expanse, still searching for that beautifully sculpted spaniel skull. Water reached my knees. I kept walking. A tiny wave licked at my thighs.

Kalli! I silently screamed. *Where the hell are you?*

And there she was. At my elbow. Casually paddling back to shore with a goofy grin on her muzzle.

"What the hell—?"

She ignored me, regaining her footing on the beach and shaking herself thoroughly as only a soaked dog can.

"Kalli!"

Hmmm? Don't you know dogs swim naturally? My only regret is I had to come back before I wanted to. And that's your fault.

What were you thinking, coming in after me when you can't swim? Honestly, humans can be so stupid at times. And I was having serious fun, too.

You should be ashamed of yourself.

WINNING BY A NOSE

Ultimate fun for Kalli meant utilizing her native-born talent: tracking. We watched her perfect this skill almost every minute of every day. After all, each step she took was an opportunity to meet a new smell, and she was the consummate opportunist. But it was when she picked up the odor of squirrel in an urban park that she was in top form.

The green belts bordering the lakefront north of Chicago boasted some of the finest squirrel specimens in the area. And each small mammal seemed devoted to taunting our spaniel by leaving its scent on the ground.

One beautiful June afternoon, Kalli and I strolled across the close-clipped grass south of Northwestern University campus. Trotting in front of me, Kalli swept her nose along the ground in a casual motion. Suddenly, she froze in place, and her stub tail wagged at the speed of light.

Without lifting her nose, she tore across the grass, zig-zagging at sharp angles, pausing to freeze and send one sharp "woof" in the air before plunging her nose into the lawn once more. Her butt wriggled the entire time. I was amazed an animal could keep her nose down and still move so fast without somersaulting.

Nevertheless, she carried on in this fashion, following a crazy-quilt pattern through the park that was completely indiscernible to the human eye. It appeared a stately, ancient maple tree was its focal point.

My assumption that the squirrel—whose scent she was tracking—had climbed this tree, was confirmed when I glanced up into the leafy boughs to see the critter staring down at us. It began chattering at me.

"This dog is out for your tail," I told him. "I'd stay up there, if you know what's good for you."

Meanwhile, Kalli had entered a world of her own. Still darting and weaving along the invisible trail left by the squirrel, her focus was complete. A bomb could have gone off next to her and she would have been oblivious.

My evil human mind went into overdrive. Kalli, completely distracted… What a *perfect* obedience training moment.

Yes, I did it. I called her in to me. And waited.

And waited.

I itched to repeat the command, but Kristen's instruction rang in my mind. The trainer never *ever* verbalizes a command more than once. And with good reason. Dogs stop listening. If the canine isn't going to obey the first time, the owner has a problem.

I began walking toward her, intent upon correcting her lack of response to my recall. I realized the little bugger had heard me and knew exactly what I expected from her.

With great reluctance, she elected to stop ignoring me and broke off her frenetic tracking. Slowly, she turned toward me.

Continuing in my evil vein, I waited for her to come all the way to me. When she sat in perfect front position at my feet, I ordered her to perform a "by-heel" finish.

It was then I learned the extent of her tracking obsession. My chow hound *did not* want a treat as her reward. She wanted to be released so she could continue her tracking.

Well, geesh. What do you want from me? I'm bred to follow the scent of that oversized rodent. It's one of the significant reasons I was placed on this planet. Of course it's more important than that pathetic little square of freeze-dried liver that's been sitting in your pocket waaaaaaay too long.

You know, I've really humored you long enough. The fact that you interrupted me just as I was hitting my stride trailing that beast is bad, in and of itself. But calling me in to you is a bit much, don't you think? After all, fair is fair. I don't interrupt you when you're watching one of those sappy movies. Okay, well, maybe I do. But that's different.

Right, so I'm in perfect heel position. May I go now? Please?

I looked down at Kalli. She was vibrating in place by my left leg. Shaking my head, I whispered, "Good girl. Go!"

A black-and-white blur whooshed off to the maple tree, and Kalli resumed her frantic tracking. It was then I noticed the older woman and her blue heeler puppy approaching us. The woman's face was wreathed in a big grin.

My heart sank. I knew exactly what was about to happen, and it wasn't going to be pretty. Sure enough, I heard the lady call to me, "Hello! Do you mind if my puppy plays with your dog?"

I plastered a smile on my face, which she obviously interpreted as agreement, because before I could utter a sound, she'd released her dog. The young heeler gamboled toward Kalli on powerful legs, and within seconds, had pulled up next to her.

Given the fact that Kalli is less than tolerant of other dogs most of the time, I could only imagine what she'd do if this puppy got in the way of her obsession. I held my breath, waiting for the inevitable growling and snarling, and was on my way to the pair so I could call in Kalli and avoid a scene. But to my amazement, the heeler backed away and kept its distance from her. He settled on the grass and watched Kalli, clearly fascinated with the maneuvers going on in front of him.

Kalli didn't look up, nor give any indication she was even aware of the puppy's existence.

By this time, the heeler's owner had joined me and was chuckling. "I take it your dog isn't interested in playing with Scooby at this time."

Relieved, I nodded and shrugged. "She lives to track squirrels...uninterrupted. What can I say?"

"No problem. Scooby'll figure it out. He's very intuitive. Remarkable in such a young dog. I've bred heelers for years and have never seen his like before."

The woman knew what she was talking about, I realized, as I watched the puppy continue to calmly study my dog. After a few moments, Scooby trotted off to one side of Kalli. And then the fun began, because that blue heeler began to shadow Kalli from fifteen feet away...far enough to be out of her way, yet close enough to stay abreast of her.

Scooby was phenomenal, perfectly mimicking Kalli's route as my spaniel's path twisted and turned through the park. Synchronous tracking...it should be an AKC event. And Kalli completely ignored him. The two dogs were a match made in heaven. The only question was, who would wear out first?

I never did learn the answer to that question because after ten minutes of canine poetry in motion, Scooby's owner collected her amazing puppy and left us.

...BY ANY OTHER NAME

Over the years, Kalli was characterized in many ways by many people. Her style begged for a description. My brother-in-law called her a "professional dog." A neighbor branded her "the spaniel diva." Marc delighted in identifying her as "more than a dog." But the label that stuck was the one attributed to her by Kristen: "the CEO of dogs."

Kalli earned this moniker in a most dubious way when Marc and I decided to leave the country for a two-week vacation. Kalli was a pro at boarding kennels, and normally we'd have had no problem taking her to the excellent facility in the far north suburbs we had used in the past. But two weeks seemed a long time to confine Kalli to a dog run when each day was broken up only by the occasional walk. We checked out other options.

Kristen's friend, Liz, owned two Kristen-trained Labs and ran an intimate dog boarding service in her large home on Chicago's West Side. Canine visitors lived in her house along with her family and dogs, shared family outings and play sessions in the large yard, and were treated to daily walks as requested by the owner.

Kristen assured me Kalli would do just fine in this setting, and indeed, during Kalli's overnight screening visit, Liz fell in love with my dog. Kalli was polite to her. I considered this a match made in heaven.

Buoyed by a belief in boarding success, I prepared for the trip. I painstakingly packed Kalli's food, treats, toys, special blankets, and towels. I spent hours typing up "just a few notes" about Kalli's preferences, quirks, expectations. After I'd created twelve pages—single-spaced—Marc urged me to bring the epistle to an end.

"But, I haven't told Liz about the evening treats, or—"

He placed a gentle hand on my shoulder. "Let it go, kid. Liz will be going way above and beyond the call of duty if she follows your instructions on just the first page."

Grumbling, I printed the pages, stuck them in one of ten bags accompanying Kalli to Liz's, and prepared myself for the inevitable pain of separation. Let me clarify that this pain was decidedly one-way. Kalli, in all her wonderful security, couldn't have cared less that we were leaving the country.

You guys always make sure I'm cared for. And since you've never failed me, yet, why should I assume that will change?

All this fuss just because we won't see each other for a while! And hey, I don't have a real sense of time, anyway.

At Liz's, I steeled myself for my last view of Kalli as I pulled each bag from the back of the car. To her credit, Liz managed to keep a straight face as I began piling bundles on the worn wood floor of her wraparound front porch. "Better to leave them out here and give Kalli

a quick good-bye," she directed me. "It's easier for you that way." She'd already figured out I was the one in danger of losing control of my emotions. And she was so right.

One by one, the bags filled the empty space around the wicker furniture. After I'd unloaded the last one, Liz smiled and escorted me to my car with a gentle hand on my elbow. I swallowed the knot of emotions stuck in my throat and pulled out into traffic. I stole a glance in my rearview mirror in time to see that Kalli wasn't even looking in my direction as I drove away. She was too intent upon the treat in Liz's hand. I reflected the woman really knew how to bond with my animal, shrugged off the impending tears, and drove home so I could begin packing for the humans.

Liz had assured me I could call every day while we were gone. She offered me the service of a daily diary describing Kalli's adventures I could read at my leisure upon my return home. I resigned myself to these small comforts.

Once in London, I called Liz. She brimmed with great news. Kalli was having a wonderful time. They loved her. All was well. Enjoy your vacation.

After the first few days, I began to take baby steps toward doing just that. I decided to take a page from Marc's book and not obsess about Kalli every minute of the trip. After all, Marc had supreme confidence in Kalli's ability to adjust to any situation. And he trusted me to make the very best arrangements for her. So, he was a happy camper. I managed to evolve into a not-quite-as-happy-but-reasonably-okay camper.

My only dicey moments occurred when I saw spaniels as Marc and I wandered around the city. Turns out cocker spaniels (they don't include the reference to "English" since that's the product of an American perspective) are very popular in London, so I had plenty of practice soothing my separation anxiety throughout the two weeks.

I was just getting the knack of the whole I-can-temporarily-exist-without-my-dog thing when it was time to return home. Once the limo dropped us off at the house and our suitcases were safely tucked into the front hall, I couldn't get to Kalli fast enough.

I hid my smile as Marc drove us to Liz's. Usually a driver who pushed the speed limit only to a modest degree, he drove down Lake Shore Drive toward the West Side at a speed that would have impressed a NASCAR driver.

We pulled in front of Liz's house, and I bounded out of the car before Marc could shut off the engine. Liz was ready for us. Kalli's bags were packed and sitting in the same spot where I'd left them. I shrugged off a flash of paranoia that wondered if Liz had even opened them. Perhaps they'd been sitting there the entire two weeks of our trip. But no, the food was gone; the treat bag was nearly empty. I took a deep breath and dropped to the floor inside Liz's house to give my wriggling dog a huge hug. She'd never looked better.

Geesh, Mom. I'm glad to see you, too, but your emotions are a bit over the top, aren't they? You're going to strangle me. Still, I suppose I can find it in my heart to forgive you.

My attention snapped away from Kalli when I caught part of Marc's conversation with Liz that was going on behind my back. I heard Marc say, "I'm so sorry that happened."

"What?" I turned to face them. Liz's eyes avoided mine. My stomach fell. Something had gone wrong. "Is there a problem? Is Kalli okay? She looks okay."

Liz sighed and shook her head. "Kalli is great. I was just telling Marc her visit turned out to have some...unexpected consequences."

I froze.

"Turns out our little dog is quite the diva." The sparkle in Marc's eyes didn't alleviate my concern. "She ruled the roost while we were gone."

Liz sighed again. "Well, she was just being herself. Unfortunately, we weren't prepared for it." She looked up at me. "She's a wonderful dog, Laura. I'm probably the one at fault here. I'm just not an assertive person. I don't have to be. My dogs are all very passive and most of my clients' dogs are, too. It took Kalli just a few days to figure that out. And then she...well...she took over."

"Took over?" My stomach started doing flip-flops in rhythm with my pounding heart.

"Especially around meal times." Liz chuckled softly. "Kalli ate her dinner, then proceeded to eat all the other dogs' meals, too. And they let her. Eventually, I ended up feeding her at a different time and then occupying her while Charlie fed the rest of the dogs." She shrugged. "It was the only way we could get food into the others."

"Oh, my God!" I groaned. "I'm so sorr—"

Liz cut me off with a wave of her hand. "Don't apologize. Kalli wanted a firm hand, and I wasn't prepared to give her one. Like I said, it was my responsibility." She paused and smiled. "Actually, it was kinda entertaining. Eventually she reorganized all the meal times for both dogs *and* humans. Then the playtimes got shuffled about. And the treats… Well, you get the picture. Before I knew it, we were all tiptoeing around her. Not that she was *physically* aggressive. Let's just say the dog knows what she wants, when she wants it."

I sank onto a chair and felt Kalli's nose bumping against my leg. I looked into her eyes, and for once, didn't find their glint of mischief endearing.

Hey! You left me, and I was thrown into this wacky household. They're terribly disorganized, you know? And no one took charge. Humph! I'd like to see them survive out in the wild for two seconds. No respect for the pack structure at all. Someone had to step in and whip them into shape. It was the very least I could do. And I did it for their own good, really.

I thought you'd be proud of me.

Anyway, I'm glad you're back because now that my work is done here, I'm really bored. Can we go home? Pleeeeeaase?

Writing the check to Liz with a shaky hand, I bit my lip to keep myself from apologizing one more time. I couldn't get out of there fast enough.

Kalli settled into her nest of towels in the car's backseat as if nothing untoward had happened, which, if I think about the situation from her perspective, was exactly the case. With a contented sigh, she closed her eyes and fell fast asleep.

One of the first things I did upon arriving home was call Kristen. I was still smarting from Liz's report and seriously needed a reality check.

Kristen's first reaction to my story was laughter—full-throated, belly-clenching laughter that went on for some minutes. When she was finally able to speak, she immediately set my mind to rest.

"Look, Kalli is a pistol. We all know that. She's the CEO of dogs. Truly. And when she's with people she doesn't feel are in control, she'll step in and fill the gap. Some of that is normal, instinctive behavior of a pack animal. In the wild, their survival depends upon a tight hierarchy in which every member has a role and understands that role. Now, in Kalli's case, she's taken that instinct to a level of sophistication most dogs don't have."

CEO of dogs? Sophistication? I shook my head and held my tongue.

Kristen seemed to sense my turmoil and went on. "You guys didn't do anything wrong with her, Laura. She's being…herself. This is a dog who doesn't suffer fools lightly. Liz didn't stand up to her and paid the price. That's the mark of a smart animal who knows who she is and how to get what she wants."

"But all the training, Kristen!"

"Yeah, well, she obeys when you give her a command, right?"

"Right." I winced at my little-girl voice.

"Okay, so what's the problem? You've earned her respect. And that respect means she'll obey you. If Liz had exerted herself, Kalli would have been fine in her home."

"She didn't get along with the other dogs, either."

"She's an only child. She's not used to sharing."

"But we've socialized her…taken her to classes and play groups."

"How did the play groups work out?"

I took a deep breath. "Not very well, unless the goal was to have Kalli locate our car in the parking lot."

Kristen chuckled. "Exactly."

"Kristen, I really don't want my dog acting like a spoiled brat who can't get along with other dogs. That just isn't cool on so many levels. So how do we handle the only-dog thing?"

"Why don't you have Kalli stay with us next time you leave on vacation? We'll put her in our board-and-train program with the other dogs and work on her."

Which is exactly what we did a few months later. We left Kalli with Kristen for a long weekend when we took a jaunt up to a bed-and-breakfast in Door County, Wisconsin.

We returned to Evanston wondering how much Kristen had achieved with Kalli in such a short time. As soon as we pulled up to Kristen's home, we found out. Before us, Kalli romped in the spacious side yard with four other dogs. That, in and of itself, wasn't remarkable. But when we saw our dog happily share a ball with Kristen's Lab, Darcy, we froze to the spot on the sidewalk.

Laughter broke our fascinated trance. We hadn't even noticed Kristen approach us. "Quite the change in your little CEO, huh?"

"No kidding," I breathed.

Marc wrapped an arm around Kristen's shoulder. "You're a miracle worker."

"Not at all," Kristen responded in her usual brisk voice. "Just have to know what buttons to push. Kalli's an extremely bright dog. Doesn't take much for her to 'get it.'"

"So, what happened?" I asked.

Kristen shrugged as she escorted us into her house. "Nothing too remarkable, really." She smiled. "I can tell by the expression on your face that you don't believe me."

Marc and I sank into armchairs in her living room and waited for the report.

"Not to take away from Kalli's brilliance, but she can be predictable. The first few hours she was here, Kalli was low-key, scouting the situation. Testing the waters, if you will. Signs of trouble began over the water dish in the yard. I have a big communal bowl back by the garage. Dogs who stay with me have to learn to share it with the others."

"Oh, no." I could just imagine what Kristen was about to say.

She nodded. "Yup. You guessed it. Kalli took over and guarded it from the other dogs. I decided to give her a chance to figure out what I wanted without becoming too heavy-handed." Kristen chuckled. "That didn't work. In fact, it made matters worse because Kalli actually thought she'd found a chink in my armor."

"So, what happened next?" Marc smiled broadly at our friend.

Kristen answered in casual tones. "I alpha-rolled her."

"You—what?" I squeaked.

The training technique of "alpha-rolling" a dog is controversial. First popularized by the Monks of Skete in their best-selling book, *How to Be Your Dog's Best Friend,* it consists of the trainer flipping a dog onto its back and holding it in place until the dog relaxes and submits to the passive position. Supposedly, this action mimics the manner in which canines establish dominance within the pack structure and the way a mother dog disciplines her puppy. Thus, the trainer is established as boss and regains control over the dog.

Many detractors in the training world believe this technique mimics a situation in which the dominant dog is pinning the other animal, intent upon killing it. Those same critics theorize that the restrained dog will fight for its life, making the situation dangerous for the trainer. Many also believe this process traumatizes the downed dog. For these reasons, the technique has fallen from favor.

Kristen obviously noticed my shock, because she replied, "I know, it's an extreme thing to do. But gaining the cooperation of some dogs is harder than others. I would never roll a passive dog. Kalli, however, is solid and secure and can take it. It was the quickest way to get her attention and keep it. I wasn't rough with her and didn't hold her down for long. Hell, it didn't take long. Kalli got the message immediately and submitted within seconds." Kristen shrugged. "And then it was over. I let her up, and Kalli started romping with the other dogs as if nothing had happened."

"What about the water dish?" I asked.

Kristen laughed. "That was priceless. Pure Kalli. The next time I looked up, the dogs were gathering around the water and Kalli had positioned herself behind Darcy, waiting her turn."

"Huh?" I'm always eloquent when profoundly surprised.

"Yup. She reminded me of a kid waiting in line for the drinking fountain in an elementary school hallway. She sat patiently behind Darcy until all the other dogs had had their water. Then she calmly drank her fill. And that's what she did the rest of the time." Kristen shook her head. "She's something."

"Doesn't sound like the actions of a CEO to me." Marc chuckled.

"Actually, it does if you think about it." Kristen turned to him. "A good leader knows how to read a situation accurately and determine the best course of action within the constraints of that situation. Kalli reasoned out what was going on and elected to back off. The consequence of not doing that outweighed the benefit of continuing to guard the water. Like I said…pure Kalli…the CEO of dogs."

Kalli would soon acquire yet another name: Certified Therapy Dog. But canine and humans had many challenges and hurdles to clear before that moniker was earned.

CARLY'S GROUP

Therapy work for Kalli and me began on a sunny spring day during our daily walk. We'd decided to visit one of our favorite lakefront parks, whereupon my dog immediately began tracking squirrels.

The particular patch of ground Kalli had elected to work ran beside the street. Not that it was a busy thoroughfare, but I knew the rare car could present a danger to my distracted dog. I kept a sharp eye on the vicinity. In doing so, I noticed an elderly lady sitting in a wheelchair under a tree not too far from Kalli's target area. A nurse hovered behind the woman with a protective hand on the back of the chair. The geriatric glowered at Kalli, the outward expression of a black mood obvious from my vantage point twenty feet away. But she was also attentive, studying my dog.

"No street!" I bellowed as the squirrel Kalli chased dashed across the road.

To her credit, Kalli came to a screeching halt, planted her rear end on the curb, and looked back at me.

Do you know what obeying your stupid command just cost me? I had that mangy beast in my sights. I could have had him in two seconds. You completely blew this for me.

Okaaay. So as long as you've stopped me, the least you can do is feed me. Where's my treat? And after the food, a bit of praise wouldn't hurt.

On cue, I obediently chimed, "Good girl," and passed over the liver morsel.

I looked up to see the hint of a smile flash across the face of the chair-bound lady, only to immediately disappear in the gloom of a deep frown.

Kalli went back to work, her coursing bringing her ever closer to the wheelchair observer and her nurse. I elected to remain silent and not cramp Kalli's style yet again, unless she moved too close to the pair. Besides, Kalli had a huge park to work. The odds of her crowding the women were long.

I should have remembered that the odds were always in Kalli's favor. After all, my dog played percentages using her own rules. Sure enough, within seconds she was darting only a few yards from the wheelchair. I had opened my mouth to issue the recall command when, of her own volition, Kalli stopped tracking in mid-stride. She looked at the elderly lady with a goofy grin on her face, then padded over to her. Kalli's calm was remarkable since she'd been racing around like a maniac just a minute before.

I arrived on the scene in time to see the woman's gaze lock on Kalli, who now stood quietly a few feet in front of the wheelchair. The elderly lady leaned precariously toward my dog, her scowl replaced by a look of curiosity.

By this time, I'd snapped the leash on Kalli and felt a bit more in control. I turned to the woman and asked, "Would you like to say hello to my dog? She's very friendly." I glanced at the nurse and received a confirming nod.

The woman was silent, but her face communicated volumes to me as a slight smile pierced her wrinkled face.

"Kalli, sit." I said this a bit uncertainly, unsure of the dynamics at play between the two. Was I making a mistake by allowing them to interact?

Kalli displayed no such uncertainty. With polished style, she settled herself at the woman's feet and continued to gaze up at her with wise spaniel eyes. A quivering hand extended toward Kalli. My dog stretched her neck so the top of her head could meet the shaky fingertips.

"Her name is Kalli?" came the quavering voice. "Such a pretty name."

I noticed tears in the nurse's eyes. "Is everything all right?" I asked her.

"Oh, more than all right. You have no idea. She doesn't speak often these days, so this is very special," the younger woman murmured.

Her charge ignored these words, her attention on my dog. Kalli was licking her hand. The woman's smile broadened. "My dog used to lick my hand," she said in soft tones.

"Is she bothering you?" I asked.

"Oh, no. She reminds me so much of Sandy. She's a dog I had when I was a little girl. Haven't thought about her in years. What kind of dog is this?"

After I'd recited my English Cocker 101 speech, the woman continued to ask me about Kalli, growing more animated as she did so. I realized something enchanting was unfolding before my eyes.

Wow. This woman really needed me, Mom. I feel as if I'm connecting with her and Sandy—that mutt she had when she was a girl. She feels...hmmm, I'm not sure how to describe this...lighter. Does that make sense? As if she's been carrying around these heavy bags...like the stuff you and Daddy use when you leave me to go on one of your trips. What do you call it? Aaaah, luggage. That's it! It's luggage on her shoulders. No wait. I think you guys refer to it as baggage. Well, whatever you want to call it, the important thing is that her back is bowed from it, and she hurts. But petting me had this weird effect on her. Like someone took a bunch of those bags and tossed them away, so they're no longer attached to her. That's what Sandy used to do for her. I'm like the stand-in for that dog.

I'm not even going to be insulted she would compare me with that stupid little thing. I just want you to know I gave up my smells for this. I guess it was worth it.

By the way...I'm ready for my next treat. I'd say I've earned it.

Not long after our encounter with the elderly lady in the park, Kalli and I relaxed in the kitchen a few minutes before dinnertime. Normally, we'd be sitting on the back patio at that time of day, but a storm raged through our neighborhood, wind whipping thick sheets of rain across the windows. It was a good time for a gin-and-tonic at the table, or a rawhide chew on the floor, depending upon whether you were human or canine.

Sipping my lime-infused beverage, I idly flipped through the latest edition of *AKC Gazette*. Midpoint in the magazine was an article describing the activities of an animal-assisted therapy group. With the memory of Kalli interacting with the wheelchair-bound geriatric fresh in my mind, I began reading the piece with interest. My attention perked up when I realized the organization operated in the Chicago area. As I scanned the text and accompanying photographs of the exploits of Carly's Group, I noticed a familiar face in one of the pictures. Kristen was a member of the organization.

I reached for the phone and called her.

She laughed at my amazement. "I thought I'd mentioned this to you. Yup, I've been involved with Carly's Group since it started a few years ago. I run the training and testing sessions, and manage one of the projects. It's called 'Urban Sisters,' and I totally love it." She paused, then added, "You know…we have an opening for another dog. Kalli would be perfect. Are you interested?"

"You've got to be kidding! My crazo dog in a therapy organization?"

"Not kidding at all," came the brisk response. "Kalli would be a great addition to the team. You've trained her within an inch of her life, so she'll pass the test with no problem. And her high energy is exactly what we need."

"Tell me about Urban Sisters."

"We hook into a drug rehabilitation program for teenage girls. Takes place in a residence facility on the near West Side. We show up each Tuesday evening for ten-week stints with a team of four certified dogs and their handlers. And we let the girls work with the dogs."

"How work with them?"

"We turn over the leashes to them and show them how to give the dogs basic obedience commands. After a few weeks, we bring in agility equipment. You guys are already familiar with the routine because we've done it in class before."

"So…some jumps and the tunnel?"

"Exactly. We also use a Hula hoop, which is hilarious. I bet Kalli would love it. Anyway, the girls put the dogs through their paces. Near the end of the ten-week session, we take everyone to a do-it-yourself grooming place, and the girls wash and dry the dogs." Kristen chuckled. "They even brush their teeth. It's lots of fun…water and soap suds everywhere, tons of giggling and great photographs. It's very therapeutic for the girls. And doesn't do us any harm, either."

She went on in a serious voice. "You see, we link their work with the dogs to their twelve-step program. So they see consistent patterns of service, commitment, and responsibility in everything they do during the Tuesday night sessions. It's all about supporting their rehab. Seriously, Kalli would be ideal. We have a training/testing session coming up in a few weeks. I'll give you a briefing sheet at our next class. Look it over and let me know if you'd like to participate."

I hung up the phone after promising Kristen I'd do just that.

My first step was to research Carly's Group. Hey, that's what I do…research stuff. I discovered the organization sent out dog/handler teams to a large network of rehabilitation centers, agencies, and hospitals throughout the Chicago area.

Patients with limited physical and verbal skills engaged in such exercises as moving with the therapy dog as it heeled, brushing and petting it, and working with the dog as it sat, laid down, retrieved balls, and jumped over obstacles. These activities increased the patients' coordination, strength, range of motion, standing balance, and speech, as well as their incentive to achieve.

Other programs targeted young people who were juvenile sex offenders, or recovering from substance abuse like the teens participating in Urban Sisters. Carly's Group activities were designed to help these special clients develop higher self-esteem, confidence, self-control, and patience.

Dogs of all shapes, sizes, and breeds were encouraged to participate. They had to pass the stringent test first, however. Based on guidelines provided by Therapy Dogs International and following the pattern of the CGC certification exam, the test was something I'd soon learn about firsthand. I decided to volunteer as an assistant for the upcoming session.

On test day, twenty dogs with their nervous owners trooped into the gymnasium of a mammoth rehabilitation facility on Chicago's West Side. I volunteered as the "friendly stranger" in an exercise much like a CGC activity. My job was to wait for the handler to heel the dog to me, at which time I greeted the dog, then ran my hands across it as a quick examination, followed by a few strokes of a grooming brush.

As I watched the activity around me, I began to feel quite smug about Kalli's ability to pass muster at the next exam. After all, we'd nailed the CGC test. My arrogant eye noted every misstep around me. Each errant wiggle, tug on a leash, startled yelp after the "loud noise" exercise sparked my inner snicker. Nervous handlers who confused their dogs with garbled commands engendered my contempt. I mentally rolled my eyes at the poodle who jumped up during the long down-stay.

I waltzed out of the session with a sense of superiority. My dog would sail through the test with grace and ease. It would be a piece of cake for her.

One Friday evening, Marc returned home after another of what seemed like an endless series of business trips to find me looking at the test schedule. I jumped up to give him a hug and a kiss, then returned to the object of my obsession. Marc set down his suit bag and walked behind me to read over my shoulder. I was just discovering the next test was two months away. There was plenty of time to pass it and begin participating in the Urban Sisters activities in the fall.

The reality of what Kalli and I contemplated, and the importance it held for me, suddenly hit me between the eyes. Indeed, I hadn't realized the true depth of my emotions about therapy work until that moment. To share my dog with others who needed to receive her gifts seemed almost spiritual to me. My gut tightened. Nerves jumped around my jaw bone.

"What's wrong, Laura?" Marc settled into the chair opposite me with a healthy scotch and scrutinized me as only he could. "I thought you wanted to become part of Carly's Group. The test is coming up soon. That's a good thing. Right?"

I mentally shook my head. Life was so much easier for him than it was for me. Marc approached each challenge with a calm and aplomb that continued to mystify and impress me, even after years of marriage. To him, the situation before me was straightforward: drill Kalli, pass the test, start working with Urban Sisters.

Simple.

Kalli and I continued our obedience classes, and I worked her within an inch of her life. My desire to join Carly's Group began to outweigh common sense. I lost hold on the reality of the situation, making the goal of passing the test a much bigger deal than it really was. I could feel my nerves jangling down the leash. Kalli appeared to ignore them. I began to feel a spark of hope. Maybe we...okay, I...could actually pull this off.

Test day extinguished the spark. I was lost to my anxiety as we entered the brightly lit gymnasium. Unfortunately, Kalli mirrored my extreme emotions and was a hyper mess as she faced a new room, a new set of dogs and humans, new smells, and new sounds. Her tracking dog instincts hit the stratosphere. I have never, ever, seen her rear end wriggle that much. It wasn't so much a blur as it was a whirlwind with its own center of gravity.

While she sat and laid down on command, recalled with a proper front and finish, and was nonplused when I left her alone for the requisite five minutes, her heeling was nonexistent. She was up and bounding around the room during the sit-stay and down-stay. Hell, she made the poodle I'd pitied during my first exposure to the test look like a champ.

Every exercise involving another person—whether the volunteer was shaking my hand, petting Kalli, or brushing her—sent her into orbit. I eyed her with amazement. Never had I seen her so out of control.

Hey! I may be an amazingly brilliant and miraculous dog, but I have my limits. You're a wreck, so I'm a wreck. That's the way it goes. Besides, we both have lessons to learn here. You have to face it, you've been crazed about this test for a long time. So, we're about to fail it gloriously. And when we do, we can go home, regroup, and figure out a better way to approach the whole thing.

Sound like a plan, Mom?

Mom?

Oh, brother. She's not even listening to me...too busy wallowing in shame. And she's not even ashamed of me, which would be a totally fair reaction on her part. She's ashamed of herself. Sometimes, she really is too much. And not even a spaniel with my amazing gifts can help that.

Well, I'm not giving up on her now. Clearly, I have some serious work ahead of me. Sighhhhh.

With Kristen's upbeat "You'll get it next time" ringing in my ears, I slunk out of the testing facility with Kalli trotting proudly beside me. I couldn't help glaring at her. How could she be so damned *happy?* We'd failed. That was nothing to be cheerful about.

In the back of my mind, I realized there had to be a better way of approaching a challenge. Being consumed with anxiety didn't seem to be the optimal attitude to bring to the table. I resolved to find a positive coping mechanism for the next test. And that resolve, coupled with Kalli's ridiculously high spirits, began to seep through the cracks of my depression. After all, we had another shot at it. And then, we'd be calm and assured and together and…

My cautious optimism disappeared the minute we got home. But a sense of purpose had begun to grow in the midst of the gloom. It was time to take action, begin anew. I stalked to the phone and called Kalli's breeder.

"Sounds like the problem was at the other end of the leash," Pam said in brisk tones. Geesh, what was it about all these professional dog people with their briskness?

"You're just saying that because you brought Kalli into the world," I said, shuddering at my weak attempt at a joke. It was times like this when I really wished I could keep my mouth shut.

"Not at all." Clearly, her briskness had overwhelmed her sense of humor.

"You've trained Kalli well," Pam went on. "She knows her stuff. Now, you need to figure out how to showcase her. Once you do that and calm down, you'll both be fine."

Couldn't argue with that.

I sat at my computer trading emails with other spaniel enthusiasts, sharing my day's disappointment. One of them suggested I investigate the work of Jane Savoie. An Olympic dressage equestrian, Jane had created a sports psychology system born from lessons she'd learned as she overcame anxiety in the face of challenges. She counsels that one's thoughts—the types of things you say to yourself—create an attitude that directly leads to success or failure. Each person has a choice to function within a positive or negative framework.

Made sense to me. The next morning, I purchased a recording of the program, *That Winning Feeling,* and spent the afternoon and evening learning Savoie's visualization techniques.

At one point that night, just before bedtime, I looked down from my reading chair to see Kalli sitting in front of me, staring into my face. I tried to interpret her expression. Boredom? Annoyance that we hadn't taken our usual hour-long walk? I finally settled on curiosity. She sensed something was up and being a narcissist, assumed the focus of my attention had something to do with her.

"Just doing homework," I told her, holding up my cassette player. "This is going to help us with Carly's Group."

She yawned and lay down.

I certainly hope it will help you, Mom. God knows, you've been a wreck. What is it about this Carly's Group thing that's so important, anyway? I mean, dogs are put on the planet to help process the emotions of humans. That's our job, and we start doing it from the moment we're born. Are you guys just figuring that out? Is that what this organization is all about? Setting me up in a place where I can help other humans? Do you really think it's necessary?

Geeeeesh. As if I don't have my hands full with you and Daddy.

Oh, boy. Wait a minute here. I just figured out what's going on. This is about that old lady in the park, isn't it? You think something special happened, and you want me to do the same thing with other people.

Hmmmm. I'm not sure how I feel about that. But then again, I'm here for you. So if you want me involved in some group that does...what did you call it? Oh, yeah, therapy work... Then, I'll do what you ask. Like I said, that's my job.

Right now, I require rest. Looks like I'm going to need it.

As I watched Kalli settle into a peaceful nap at my feet, I began implementing the tools I'd just learned from Savoie's tape. Creating a positive mental picture of Kalli and me at the next Carly's Group session, I took every step of that test in my head, with Kalli by my side in perfect control. I was relaxed, having fun. And we passed with flying colors.

I reflected on how I felt after completing the visualization. For the first time in weeks, true relaxation drifted through my body. A delightful self-assurance followed in its wake.

In that moment, I chose success.

Kalli and I went back to work with revived energy and a new spirit. A miraculous shift took place in my attitude as I altered the nature of my thoughts over the next few months. Whenever I caught myself in a place of negativity, I moved into a mental picture of glorious success. Around this image I wrapped a simple mantra for Kalli and me: "We're passing the test." I whispered the mantra to Kalli as we heeled down the neighborhood sidewalks, speaking the words in a little rhythm that synced with the pattern of our steps. I spoke it aloud in the parks when Kalli performed a perfect recall, front, and finish. I sang it to Kalli when I tucked her into her sleeping crate at night. I hummed it to myself as I vacuumed, made dinner, unloaded the dishwasher. And with each utterance, my belief in that positive affirmation grew. I simply didn't allow myself to do anything else but believe all would be well. During those months of preparation, Kalli and I passed the Carly's Group test hundreds of times in my head.

On a Saturday morning in late September, Marc and I packed Kalli's gear—poop bags, tons of liver treats, leash, training collar, and paper towels—and prepared to hit the road. Our destination was the rehabilitation facility on Chicago's West Side.

It was test day. It was also my birthday.

"You're going to be fine, you know," Marc said in encouraging tones as we pulled away from the house. "You guys have worked really hard. There's no reason why you can't pass the test."

I laughed. "You have no idea."

"Hey, I'm proud of you." He reached out to cradle my hand in his. "You've transformed yourself. Those imaging exercises have made a real difference. Even I can see it. And you know how oblivious I can be." He chuckled.

As Marc continued a steady stream of light chatter designed to calm and support me, I settled back in my seat and watched the world pass outside the car window. The weather was picture perfect…one of those amazing fall days that only Chicago can deliver. Lake Michigan stretched along the Drive in a perfect blanket of blue. Seagulls drifted overhead, flashes of white in an azure sky. Windows of the high-rises bordering one side of the Drive twinkled with reflective sunlight.

Crisp, clear air wafted around the stately Hancock Building and ornate Drake Hotel, which rose before us as we motored toward the heart of the city. Continuing south, the magnificent skyline of downtown Chicago unfolded its rich architectural tapestry. Traffic was light, and the road stretched before us in organized strips of lanes, pointing the way to our destiny. Or, so I fantasized.

Turning off the Drive and heading into the gritty West Side, the vacant lots of Lawndale—once a teeming business district that had been destroyed during the '60's riots—hinted of promise and potential for future commerce. Centered within a positive state of mind, I felt those prospects hovering just beyond the neighborhood's reach, waiting, beckoning. Ready to be realized.

Excitement coursed through me. That morning was all about a thrilling future, whether it belonged to an urban neighborhood, or a dog and her handler.

By the time we pulled into the facility's parking lot, I was buzzing with joy. For the briefest moment, I paused to revel in the contrast between my current mood and the soul-gripping anxiety I'd experienced at the test a few months before. I looked over my shoulder and caught Kalli in the heart of a solid nap. She snored softly.

Marc chuckled and caught my eye. "She is the poster child for cozy, isn't she?"

I nodded. "No one does it like Kalli."

Apparently sensing our scrutiny, she opened her eyes and flicked her eyebrows at us. Yawning, she stood and stretched in a leisurely, feline sort of way, then walked to the door and awaited her release from the car.

Yup. We were ready.

The test unfolded before us in the same festive style as had our trip down Lake Shore Drive. Kalli was at the top of her form. When the dogs lined up side by side with the command to lie down and stay, a poodle next to her kept wandering toward his handler. If Kalli had been reflecting a nervous, basket-case owner, she would have been up and wiggling after this dog in a heartbeat. But on that day, as I stayed true to a positive outlook, Kalli merely sighed at the poodle and sprawled on the floor, froggy-style, looking up at all of us with her big brown eyes.

Pathetic dog. Clearly no discipline or style at all. Perhaps a few more classes would help him. Or his daddy could have learned lessons like Mommy did. What a transformation in her! She's worked really hard at changing herself, and I'm proud. Look at her! Calm and collected, standing over there. She's knows I'm not going anywhere until she tells me to. With her new attitude, I'd do anything for her. She's going to pass this test and join Carly's Group, just like she wanted to.

Oh, and yeah…I'll tag along.

Kalli breezed through the remainder of the test with flying colors. She held all her stays while I shook hands with other people and petted their dogs, heeled by my side…everything. At the end of the session, test participants gathered at one end of the gymnasium. Kristen stood before a table across which stretched neat rows of royal blue collars and leashes. This was the official Carly's Group equipment worn by all certified therapy dogs.

The magnitude of the moment hit me between the eyes as I stared at the sea of blue. A corner of my mind screamed, "We did it! We did it!"

Kalli yawned.

And when Kristen handed me Kalli's leash and collar with the engraved "Carly's Group" tags attached to them, I almost started crying. Never could I have imagined a better birthday gift. Seemingly oblivious to the drama of the moment, Kalli decided to wiggle her way across the room to say "hello" to the poodle.

A PROFESSIONAL THERAPY DOG

A few weeks later, Kalli and I jumped into the Urban Sisters program with all feet and paws. A team of three other dogs joined us: Macey, the Rottweiler; Sadie, the English springer spaniel; and Coco, the Great Dane. Their humans came along for the ride.

Our destination on that Tuesday evening was a residence facility on Chicago's near West Side. The complex housed teens court-mandated to participate in an intensive twelve-step program for drug abuse recovery. Dogs and owners rendezvoused in the facility's parking lot tucked under the Elevated train tracks running along Lake Street.

With the rumbling, screaming trains careening over our heads, we took stock of the area. In the heart of gang territory, the facility building offered a cheerful note on a streetscape weighted down with oppressive graffiti and rubbish-strewn alleys. Homeless folks hovered in corners. Shopping carts parked by their sides overflowed with their possessions. Their nervous eyes flickered over our dogs as we passed them.

I glanced at Kalli. She was taking the new environment in stride as only a well-adjusted, secure dog can. After a quick look at the trains rushing above her, she returned to her instinctive roots and put her nose to work. So fascinated was she by the new scents, she followed my directions automatically, her nose hovering barely an inch from the pavement the entire time.

For once, I actually understood her obsession. The odors of this time-worn neighborhood assaulted my senses, too. The stench of urine, rotting food, and car exhaust blasted us in oppressive waves. It was mitigated by a few brave tendrils of sweetness from autumn roses surviving in a nearby garden. Part of an urban planning "renewal" project, this tiny park positioned across the street from the facility would become my refuge during our visits to the area in the months and years ahead.

Pausing on a corner as we waited for the traffic light to change, Kalli set her target on a lamp post and pressed her nose against every inch of the filthy metal base. Behind me, I heard Kristen chuckle. I turned to see her maneuvering Coco around a bike chained to a parking meter post. "Kalli certainly makes her priorities clear, doesn't she?"

"Always," I said with a smile. From the moment we'd climbed out of the car, Kalli had stayed true to a private agenda. I couldn't help but wonder if she would tear herself away from her own business long enough to participate in the evening's activities.

Kristen and I guided our dogs across the street. I glanced over my shoulder to see the other dog-and-handler teams lagging behind us. They'd missed the light, so Kristen and I waited for them in front of the rehab center.

I looked down the sidewalk in time to see a pair of little boys barreling toward us on their bicycles. Their current course and speed had them landing in our laps with the inevitability of targeted cruise missiles. But when they spotted us, they braked to a dusty stop inches from our feet.

"Oh, man. Check out the huge dog. It's like a horse or something." The smaller of the two boys flung himself off his bike and scrambled toward Coco.

His companion proved to be more circumspect, staying on his bike and edging closer to us. Eyes glued to the animals, he paid no attention to where his bike was going, which I noticed immediately because the front wheel edged near Kalli's paws. I maneuvered her out of his way as I helped Kristen answer the barrage of questions spilling from his friend:

"Is it a boy or a girl?"

"How much does she eat? Gallons of food, I bet."

"Does she bite?"

Meanwhile, the bike wheel targeted Kalli. It nudged her once, then twice. The leash tugged, and I glanced down to see her attempt to maneuver away from the bike. I immediately loosened my grip on the leather strap to give her freedom of movement. With a *humph,* staring at the boy all the while, she deliberately moved next to Coco. The bike followed her as if it had developed a will of its own.

Now pressed against the Dane's side, Kalli glared at the boy and then very carefully positioned herself until she stood *underneath* Coco. It was a perfect fit. She was able to stand tall and still have inches of space between her head and Coco's tummy. The bigger dog didn't seem to notice her.

She sighed. It was a contented sort of sound. I'm sure she felt her maneuver was a success now that she was sheltered against wandering bike wheels. I could have sworn she winked at me from her safe harbor.

The paired dogs looked like canine Russian nesting dolls. Kristen caught my eye, and we burst into laughter. Only Kalli would find such an elegant solution to an annoying dilemma.

Seconds later, the team reunited and we entered the facility lobby. I dragged Kalli as she snuffled behind me. Bright neon lights hummed overhead as we approached the receptionist's counter. A young woman with a beaming smile greeted us.

"It's so great to have you guys back!" she said to us. "Ohhhhh. You have a new dog this year." Her sparkling eyes zeroed in on Kalli. "Whaaaat a cutie." She left the counter to approach us. "I'd ask if I can pet her, but that's the whole point of you being here, isn't it?" She knelt in front of Kalli, whose nose was stuffed into the tight weave of the carpet. The girl was quickly joined by a group of teenagers and adults who clustered around Kalli, oohing and aahing.

"Isn't she the cutest thing?"

"I wonder what kind of dog this is?"

"I could just eat her up, she's so darling."

I gave the collar a quick jerk to get Kalli's attention, then held her firmly in place in the "stand" position, one hand supporting her abdomen in front of her hind legs, the other wrapped around the leash and under her chin.

"Showtime, darling," I whispered to her.

Hmmm? Huh? Oh, right. I'm supposed to be working or doing something now, aren't I? And I guess you want me to stop filtering the delicious smells from this rug. You have no idea what you're asking. This is truly luscious...a whole array of scents to add to my repertoire. Everything is new. New, I tell you! I'm in doggie heaven.

Hmmmm? You're serious about this, aren't you?

Allllll right! I get it. I'll greet this woman. The sacrifices I make for you.

Wow, she really likes me. I'd almost be flattered if she weren't doing that oozing thing.

I hate oozers, but I'll tolerate her for your sake.

Kalli responded to the crowd she'd attracted in the lobby with a polite butt wriggle and a few laps of her tongue on outstretched hands. I knew my dog was disgusted, but had chosen to cooperate with me. Thus the tone was set for Kalli's involvement with Urban Sisters. She was biddable, polite, and ever-watchful for an opening to pursue her personal agenda.

An elevator took us up to the second floor and the conference room that would be the headquarters for our program activities. Kalli had never ridden in an elevator before. As the doors slid shut and the cage began rising, I eyed her with concern, not sure how she'd respond to the new experience. I needn't have worried. Other than splaying her legs to steady herself during the jerking ride, she didn't seem to find anything untoward in the event. She bounded out of the elevator as soon as the doors slid open, nose to floor. Yet another set of new smells welcomed her in the conference room. My dog was in heaven again.

Realizing Kalli needed time to greet the new round of sensory data before she'd settle to work, I stepped away from the team and gave her the freedom she craved. Around and around we trooped, sweeping from one corner to the next as Kalli crammed her face into the institutional blue carpet. Thankfully, the teens and their counselors hadn't arrived yet, and my fellow-Carly's Group handlers had already learned enough about Kalli to understand what I was doing.

I looked around me, trying to get my own bearings in the space. Harsh neon lights beat against a wall comprised of a giant whiteboard. Words scrawled across the surface by the counselors included:

"How can you be more responsible in your life?"

"Write down five things you want to do when you go home."

Personal expressions of overflowing teenage emotion were also represented on the board:

"Callista sucks."

"Roy asked me to marry him!"

"I'm going home tomorrow!"

Easels set up in two corners displayed giant sheets of paper on which were written some of the core principles of the twelve-step rehabilitation program: commitment, rewards, empowerment, trust, risks… A metal-framed conference table with a plastic surface stretched through the heart of the long rectangular space, with smaller tables and metal folding chairs lining the walls at either end.

After a few minutes, just as Kalli's frenetic pace slowed the tiniest bit, the elevator doors swept open and the air filled with female giggles, shouts, and reproving adult words. The Urban Sisters had arrived.

A mix of adults and youths stalled at the threshold. The counselors paused only briefly before they brushed past the girls to welcome us with broad smiles, hands outstretched. A chorus of introductions—the focus placed on the dogs, of course—ensued.

Six girls ranging in age from twelve to sixteen clumped together in a gaggle at the door, eyeing our dogs.

"Ooh, ooh. Would you look at the big thing?"

"It's like the dog my uncle has."

"I think the little black-and-white one is cool!"

"I ain't goin' in there!"

The two counselors, India and Sarah, turned back to their charges. "Come on in," encouraged India, a robust woman with sparkling dark eyes and a huge smile. "These animals won't hurt you."

"Well, hell. I'm not waiting," grumbled a tall, gangly girl named Rosa. She stomped into the conference room, announcing in a gruff, aggressive tone, "This is *my* dog." She wrapped her arms around Macey, the Rottweiler, without fanfare…or permission. Macey's owner, Weltha—my friend from puppy obedience class—stepped in. "Honey, you should never go up to a strange dog and handle it without asking the owner first."

Angry dark eyes snapped at her. "You're here because of us, right?"

"Right."

"So, how come we have to ask first?"

"Because some dogs can be dangerous." Sarah approached her charge with purpose.

"But this one ain't."

"True," Sarah replied in a calm voice. "But part of what you're going to be learning is the proper way to interact with all dogs. Not just trained therapy dogs."

Rosa backed away in the face of Sarah's authority. "Okay," she mumbled, stomping to a chair by the conference table and curling up in the seat.

"You'll be able to work with Macey all you want," Weltha told her in a bright voice. "But let's get everyone settled first, okay?"

Rosa's scowl answered her.

Meanwhile, four of the other girls had entered the room and, learning the lesson Rosa had offered them, were shyly asking the Carly's Group volunteers if they could pet their dogs. I looked down to see a tiny girl standing before me with complete assurance and a grin on her face. She pointed at my dog. "Who's that?"

"This is Kalli," I responded, automatically dropping to my knees next to my dog and settling her in a controlled "stand" position. I looked to India with a silent question and she responded, "That's Bettina you're talking to."

I nodded and turned to the girl, saying, "Would you like to pet her?"

Bettina's grin widened. "I guess so." She knelt next to me and stroked Kalli's head. Kalli twisted around and licked the girl's hand. Bettina giggled.

She smells funny...kinda like a stinky perfume Mom uses when she's going out with Daddy. Only this is different from Mom's...much sweeter.

Well, as misguided as this girl probably is, she seems okay. Really likes me a lot. That always helps.

Hey! You have a treat for me? No?

Oh, boy. I certainly hope Mom tells them about my treats or this is going to be a very long night.

Hmmmm? What's Mom saying? Oh, yeah. I'm a therapy dog. I have to be nice, even if I don't get food.

Geesh...more sacrifices I'm making for my humans.

As the one-sided romance between the teenager and my dog blossomed, I noticed a girl still huddled in the doorway. I smiled at her. "It's okay to come in, you know."

She shook her head.

"Kara, what's the problem?" India called to her charge.

"I ain't goin' in there." She was staring at Kalli. "They'll bite me."

"No, sweetie," I said. "These dogs are all gentle. They won't hurt you."

"Please come in now." India's assertive tone didn't allow debate.

The teenager's frightened expression shifted to annoyance as she looked at her counselor.

India said in a softer voice, "The owners are right here to make sure nothing happens. So you're safe with the dogs. Honestly."

Kara drew a huge breath and bounded into the room as if she were jumping into the deep end of a pool and couldn't swim. She careened toward the long conference table and lurched up onto it, jamming her legs under her in one fluid movement. As she tucked herself into a ball, she reminded me of a defiant young Buddha.

"Kara! What are you doing up there?" came the ever-patient voice of India.

The girl shook her head. "I ain't movin' off this table. They'll bite me. Especially that one." She jabbed an accusatory finger toward Kalli.

I threw India another silent question. The counselor shook her head and said to me, "It's because Kalli is so active. Her sudden movements can be off-putting if you're already nervous about dogs." She smiled at me. "We've seen this before. You shouldn't worry or take it personally. Actually, it's a really good thing for them to work through their fears. Your dog is already contributing to the cause."

She turned to Kara. "This is Kalli. She's a very nice dog. See how she's kissing Bettina."

I looked down to see Kalli's tongue slathering slime across Bettina's one cheek. I wasn't fooled for a minute by this seeming show of affection. Obviously, the teenager was wearing a skin cream of which Kalli approved. My dog was a sucker for cosmetics.

"That's different," came the belligerent reply. "That's Bettina."

"Kalli likes everyone. You'll see."

"No one likes me." Kara's strangled voice cut through the giggles and shouts, startling in its raw emotion.

The room fell silent, immobilized in the stark moment.

Kalli gave Bettina a final slurp and began to struggle against the hold I had on her. Instincts kicking in, I released my dog, giving her freedom of movement.

She walked up to the table where Kara cowered and play-bowed before the girl. Then she dropped her butt onto the rug and lay still, placing her muzzle on her outstretched front paws. Her stub tail bobbed back and forth as she stared up at the teen with the same steady gaze I'd noticed her using with the wheelchair-bound geriatric in the park.

For a long moment, Kara and Kalli eyed each other. A pin could have dropped on the carpet and it would have been as jolting as a gunshot. The only sound was Kalli's tail beating a steady tattoo on the rug, a heartbeat bringing new blood and warmth to a frozen child.

We all held our breath as Kara inched a tennis-shoe-clad foot toward the edge of the table. The top of the shoe extended out into the air.

I could tell Kalli was sizing up the situation. She raised an eyebrow and woofed softly.

Come on, kid. You can do this. Geesh, if my brown eyes don't get to you, who or what can? You have to give this a shot...reach for it.

Look, honey, I'm not thrilled being here myself. Haven't had a treat in forever. But, if I can hang in here, you sure can.

Yeah, I know. I can see the nightmare in your eyes...scary stuff you don't want to share. And frankly, I don't want to know about it. But this is important, and you have to pay attention to me. Now, move that foot and get your butt down here.

Kara's leg followed the movement of her foot and slowly, inch by inch, she uncurled her body until she was standing in front of my dog.

I stepped next to Kalli and grabbed the leash. "Sit," I whispered.

She slowly worked her front legs until she was in position.

"Stay."

I managed to catch Kara's eye. "Do you see how I did that with her?"

The girl nodded.

"That's what you're going to be doing in a little while." Her eyes grew wide, and I could see a mixture of emotions roiling in their depths: anger, fear, belligerence. I looked up and exchanged glances with Kristen, who nodded at me and said softly, "Go ahead, Laura. Finish it."

I gestured to Kara. "Come here, kiddo. Let's see if we can't get this dog to work for us."

She shuffled slowly to my side. I held up my hands so she could see the way in which I was grasping the leash, then I passed it to her. She took a step back as if the leather strap had morphed into a snake and was going to bite her.

I waited.

Curiosity got the better of her and with hands quivering only a little, she took the leash from me.

After adjusting her hold, I stepped away from the pair. Kara started to follow me and I stopped her. "Your place is next to your dog. She's always on your left. I have her in position, so just stand next to her. Good. Now, when you're ready, I want you to step off with your left leg and at the same time, say, 'Kalli, heel.'"

She threw me a wide-eyed look. Terror had regained control.

"You can do it."

For a long moment, Kara stood motionless next to Kalli, who sat patiently, waiting for the command. I could practically see the wheels turning in the child's head as she grappled with the situation. I wondered what she was thinking. In a quivering voice, she uttered the command.

Kalli stepped off promptly, then hesitated because her handler hadn't moved. She looked back at the teenager and raised her eyebrows again.

Okay, this isn't a solo act, kid. We're going to jump through these silly hoops together.

Oh, man. This has you really freaked, doesn't it? Hmmm. Well, a dog can only do so much. If I move, I'll break command. And yet, sometimes a few rules have to be broken to get something accomplished.

I know just what to do. Every instinct tells me what you need.

Tell you what...I'll risk getting scolded if you'll stow that fear to the side and move. Ready? Here goes...

I started toward the pair, thinking that I'd get Kara to walk with my dog if I had to kick her in the butt to do it. But before I could take action, Kalli solved the problem for me. She returned to Kara's side and gently, with what appeared to be careful intent, licked the top of Kara's shaking hand where it dangled, fingers still coiled around the leash in a death grip.

Horror shimmied through me. I was sure the teen would freak over my dog's advances. But rather than a shriek, she started to giggle...very softly at first, then louder. The sound shimmered through the air, winding its way among the girls like a ribbon loosening around a wrapped gift, touching each before moving on to the next. First one girl, then another joined Kara until the entire room erupted in laughter.

Kara transformed before our eyes. Leaning over, she cupped Kalli's muzzle with her hands, saying, "Dog, you are about the cutest damn thing I've ever seen! Ain't goin' bite me neither, I bet." She turned to me. "What am I supposed to say again?"

"Heel," I replied. "The command is, 'Kalli, heel.' Get her back in position by moving forward a few steps. She'll follow you."

In a booming voice filled with bravado, she issued her orders. Dutifully, Kalli walked by her side in perfect heel position.

"Where do I go with her?" she flung at us over her shoulder.

Kristen responded, "Take her around the room, sweetie."

"You go, girl," chimed Bettina.

Kara nodded her head sharply. "Come on, Kalli. We'll show them."

And across the carpet they marched, a triumphant pair glowing with their achievement. I held my breath at first, praying Kalli would continue to cooperate with Kara. But I needn't have worried. She maintained her decorum with style and aplomb.

"Damn," one of the girls said as the pair swept by her. "That's awesome the way that dog's doing that thing."

"Mmm hmm," echoed the teen sitting next to her. She turned to India. "Are we all going to be doing that?"

Kristen spoke up. "Oh, yes. Each and every one of you. But first, let's discuss what just happened here and get to know each other a bit better in the process."

I heard my cue. Time to bring the enchanting moment to an end. At least for that night. Which was just as well because, frankly, I was wiped after that little episode. And terribly relieved. Now I knew Kalli would work for Urban Sisters. Somewhere deep inside her brilliant canine brain, she'd recognized her role and had accepted it.

The miracle didn't end with Kara's heeling adventure. Each Tuesday night, we saw another one unfold. And it was usually the simplest activity that sparked the magic. For example, later that same night, the street-tough Bettina dissolved into tears when the Great Dane, Coco, obeyed her command and sat.

Kristen was by her side in a heartbeat. "What happened, dear? Are you all right?"

"It's just...just..."

"Just, what?"

"No one ever does what I tell 'em. Not like that, I mean." She struggled for breath. "She didn't ignore me, or anything, did she?" Bettina looked at Kristen with imploring eyes. "She really did it? It wasn't a trick, was it?"

I could see Kristen steady herself under the onslaught of the teen's poignant emotions. "No, dear. She most certainly did not ignore you, and it was no trick. I'll bet she'll listen to you one more time. Want to try telling her to lie down?"

Bettina nodded.

"You remember the command?"

Another nod, then the tremulous words rang out: "Coco? Down!"

With gentle ease, the tan giant slid to the floor, a goofy grin on her face.

"Damn!" Bettina turned to the others. "Did you see that? Did you? Did you see what happened?"

And the evening's work resumed. Later, after the girls had been ushered out of the conference room, India sat with us to discuss the events of that night's session.

"One of your greatest gifts is the simplest." She glanced at me and probably saw confusion on my face because she smiled at me and said, "I'll explain that. Now, I'm going to generalize here, so please listen to what I'm about to say within that context. We see a pattern repeat again and again with these girls. Many of them come from troubled homes in distressed areas of the city. They act out roles they've witnessed growing up. Dogs, in particular, are potent symbols of that syndrome because within the girls' environments, they're not usually loving house pets—they're large-breed animals trained to protect and fight. And they're the property of the men in the neighborhood. Women do not handle them and are brought up to fear them.

"Couple that with the fact that these girls are rarely nurtured. Or, as they say, 'listened to.' So, you ladies show up and tell them the dogs will obey them...will *listen to them*. That's powerful stuff. Whether she shows it or not, each girl is knocked out by that first experience commanding one of your dogs and seeing it respond. When they get back to their rooms, it's all they can talk about...for weeks. You've opened up a whole new world for them. You're introducing them to the concept of confidence and self-reliance...respect and self-respect."

She broke off and took a shaky breath. "Trust me. This is so much more than a simple dog-handling program." She fell silent.

Kalli yawned.

Um, Mom? The smells got old ages ago. And I'm soooo ready to go home. It's exhausting being good, especially for this long. I mean, we've been here foreeeeeeever.

Hmmmm? Right, right. You told me to lie down and stay. Sorry if I wanted to shift a little bit. Paws do fall asleep sometimes.

Oh, man. You're really sucked into all this stuff with the girls. Which means we'll be coming back? Not sure how I feel about that. Their energy is kinda all over the place. It's very different from what I'm used to with you and Daddy. Makes it hard for me to get my bearings sometimes.

Siiiiigh. I suppose I'll learn not to let it bother me. Especially since this is so important to you. But just keep in mind I'm working reaalllllly hard. And that means more treats. Got that? Look into my brown eyes and repeat after me: Moooooore treats. Moooooore treats. Moooooore...

I knew Kalli was bored with Urban Sisters. And her attitude became increasingly clear to me as the Tuesday sessions continued. Not that she did anything overtly wrong. She'd never be that obvious. Indeed, Kalli did all that was asked of her, obeying commands flawlessly, allowing herself to be manhandled by fawning teenagers, holding endless down-stays during discussions…and processing all this with typical spaniel panache. No, Kalli's boredom wove its way through each Tuesday evening in subtle touches only I, and occasionally Kristen, noticed.

Often when we took a break and Kalli wasn't on command, she'd lie with her back to us, silently defying the girls to pet her. The body language didn't communicate to the eager kids, however. Once they started working with her, they loved her, and rarely left her alone. Still, her careful positioning screamed an alarm to me.

Kalli also took every opportunity to slip out of the conference room. I thought this was a bid to explore new smells elsewhere on the floor until one evening when her intent became crystal clear. It was a busy night and a distracting one. Bettina's temper erupted when Sadie, the English springer, failed to respond to her quickly. The girl had smacked the dog on the butt. All activity came to a screeching halt. Time for a Major Discussion.

When Bettina lost her cool, Allie was heeling Kalli across the room from me. With the typical teenage attention span of a gnat, Allie apparently dropped the leash that tethered her to my dog and forgot all about her as the girl scurried toward the center of the action. Indeed, we were all riveted by the drama unfolding before us. And thus it was that a different kind of drama was unleashed without any of us noticing.

As we clustered together to talk about Bettina's behavior, I noted Allie was sitting on the floor across the room from me. She was partially obscured from my view as she hunched behind her friends. I assumed Kalli was with her.

In the midst of Bettina's dramatic soliloquy, the conference room phone rang. India glared at it. Clearly, receiving calls during a session wasn't encouraged and was especially unwelcome given the current turn of events. She hesitated, then picked up the receiver with a curt, "Yes?"

She listened for a few seconds, then spoke into the mouthpiece. "Are you kidding me? Really?" Her eyes darted around the room as if she were looking for something. "Right. Right. I'll tell her." She replaced the receiver, turned to me, and took a deep breath. "It appears Kalli is ready to go home."

"Excuse me?"

"She's downstairs, sitting by the entrance, waiting for you. Or so says our receptionist."

Anxiety coursed through me and I jumped to my feet. "Allie?" I turned toward the girl, who shrugged.

"She ain't with me."

"But you—" I wanted to yell at this child to whom I had entrusted my precious dog. How dare she be so careless? But I swallowed my angry words, aware this wasn't the time to start yet another dramatic discussion. I had a dog to retrieve.

"Looks like we have something else to talk about this evening," India said in severe tones as she glared at the teen. "This program is all about trust, Allie."

India's words faded behind me as I headed down the hallway. I punched the elevator button and waited for the cage to move from the first to second floor.

Elevator. *Elevator.*

Suddenly, it hit me that Kalli must have taken it down to the lobby. The only other way to get to the first floor was via the steps, and the stairway door connected to an alarm system. If it had been opened, the warning bell would have shrieked.

The elevator must have remained open after someone arrived on the second floor. Kalli entered the space, and the doors closed behind her. Then, it appeared as if she had been carried down to the first floor.

"Don't give it a thought. Those elevators can be weird," the receptionist assured me a minute later. "Something about the sensors picking up movement on the threshold, I think. Or some such thing." She shrugged. "I don't know how it works. All I know is I've been 'taken for a ride' more than once that way." She winked at me. "Your dog had quite an adventure."

"Yes, didn't she?" I eyed Kalli, who was staring up at me with hope in her eyes.

When I'd first arrived in the lobby, I'd been riveted by the sight of her, lying patiently by the entrance, waiting for me. She was offering only a vague wiggle of her stub tail in response to the laughing attention she was receiving from folks passing in and out of the center. If nothing else, Kalli was focused. Once she determined her objective, little distracted her, not even the admiration of humans. She was clearly planning to leave.

When I neared her, she jumped up and settled into a sit-stay by the front glass windows, her leash wrapped demurely around her. I shuddered as I had a nightmarish image of that strip of leather catching in the elevator doors and strangling her.

Shaking off my macabre thought, I arranged my face into a stern expression—I hoped. "Now, what was *that* all about, young lady?"

I'm ready to go home, Mom. How about you? It's been a long night. Pleeeeeease can we go home now? I mean, what more could you possibly have left to do up there?

Ummm? What's that? Oh, the elevator thing. You want to know how I did it. Not exactly rocket science. The doors were open and I decided to sit in there and wait for you. Very cool smells on that rug, by the way. Then, all of a sudden, the thing was shutting and I was being taken down here.

I figured it was a good thing. Right? And...well...I knew I'd get your attention, I'll admit. But, really! Something had to get through to you.

Where are you taking me? The way out is over there.

Oh, man. You have got to be kidding me. We're really going up there again?

Okaaaaaay. I'm going.

I escorted her to the conference room, where we were greeted with laughter and applause by everyone except a certain teenage girl who'd failed to attend to my dog. The ensuing conversation was intense and filled with tears. But the message of trust and responsibility was communicated to Allie that night in a way I'm sure she's never forgotten.

As for Kalli, she had also communicated a message. My attention now turned to keeping her under tighter control for the remainder of the Urban Sisters sessions. I needn't have worried. Her willingness to please and, when all was said and done, her commitment to helping the teens, overrode her boredom. It seemed once she'd made her point, she was willing to settle into the program with guarded enthusiasm.

Our involvement with Carly's Group wasn't limited to the Urban Sisters project. During one winter, Kalli and I joined Kristen and her Lab, Darcy, at a nearby West Side medical complex. In the heart of the hospital's rehab unit, we gathered with a handful of patients of varying ages recovering from strokes and surgeries. A young man named Larry took quite a shine to Kalli. He'd lost his ability to speak and the use of one side of his body as a result of a stroke, yet made his wishes very clear by moving his head and gesturing with his good arm. Drawn to Kalli's energy and nonstop activity, he gestured to his nurse that he wanted his wheelchair rolled alongside her during each session.

Working with clients in wheelchairs always presented a challenge for my dog because of her size. Standing fifteen inches tall at her shoulders and weighing twenty-seven pounds, Kalli was too large and heavy to be placed on a lap, and too short to be able to work from the floor. To solve this problem, I trained her to jump on a seat pulled alongside the wheelchair and interact with the client from this perch. As long as the furniture didn't slip under her—a non-skid bath mat accompanied us to each rehab session—she was content to follow all the standard commands from the seat. And she even deigned to sit quietly while the wheelchair patient stroked her back.

One afternoon, Larry rolled into the conference room along with three other patients and immediately gestured toward Kalli in impatient, jerky motions. His nurse and I jumped to comply with his wishes, and I settled Kalli in a chair alongside him. With his functioning arm, he patted her head.

I noticed the roll of her eyes and wondered if my energetic dog was going to cooperate with the young man. I stepped up next to her and said in bright tones, "Larry, would you like to play a game of fetch with Kalli?"

His head bobbed erratically. I took that as a nod and ordered Kalli to the floor. I placed her on a sit-stay a few feet in front of him. "Remember how we did this before, Larry?" I said in his ear. "You'll toss the ball to Kalli. She'll pick it up and sit. Then you'll call out: 'Kalli, come.' And she'll bring the ball back to you."

After another head gesture, I sent Kalli off with a hand signal. Moving behind the boy, I prepared to give her the silent signals necessary for her to fetch and return the ball independent of the confusing cues she would receive from him.

I placed the ball in Larry's functioning hand, and he threw it out into the center of the room. After a wave of my arm, Kalli trotted to it, picked it up, then turned and sat facing him.

"Okay, Larry. Tell her to return to us." And even though I knew the young man's stroke had silenced him, I added, "Say to her, 'Kalli, come!'"

I was just about to signal to her, when I heard a stuttering, strangled sound reverberate in the sterile air.

"K…k…kal. C…o…m!"

The bustling room froze. All eyes turned to the young man who hadn't made a sound in months. One of the nurses gasped.

Again, the joyful sound rang out, this time louder. "K…k…kal. C…o…m!" Larry used the hard "k" sound with gusto, the other consonants and vowels bouncing from it like the thwack of a hard rubber ball ricocheting off a wood floor.

With a start, I realized I hadn't gestured to Kalli and she wouldn't move without a recognizable signal. Yet, when I turned to her, I saw she'd responded to his second command, even though the sounds were garbled. Very purposefully, she'd stood, the ball still tucked in her mouth, and trotted to him. Without a cue from any of us, she jumped onto the chair next to him and swiveled to face him.

Larry grabbed the ball from her and threw it out again. Thus began an intense play session punctuated by the boy's joyful voice ringing in our ears. There wasn't a dry eye in the room.

"I can't believe he's making those sounds," I heard one doctor murmur behind me. "We weren't sure he'd ever talk again."

"Look at him go!" bubbled a nurse. "This truly is astonishing."

"It's the dogs," said one of the therapists. "They bring about the unimaginable, I'm telling you. Consider how frustrated Larry has been. Last night, he was so angry, he dumped his food tray onto the floor. Yet here, he's transformed. I've never seen him so enthusiastic."

"That little black-and-white dog did it," said the nurse.

"I've heard about therapy dogs, but..." The doctor seemed at a loss for words, and he let his sentence trail into the excitement of the room.

"How else do you explain the change in Larry?" the therapist asked. "We aren't able to get him this charged up unless he's with these dogs. Then, he's a different person."

The doctor shrugged. "I can't explain it."

Of course you can't explain it, you sad human person. You're not opening your mind to what your eyes are seeing.

I can tell you need some help. Listen very carefully to what I'm about to say.

I did this. Well, me and Darcy.

And it isn't a miracle. The kid was bored and needed something to jerk him out of his dark thoughts. I distracted him enough so he forgot about his troubles. He's remembering how to have fun. Don't you get it? Well, that and the healing energy I'm sending him. A little well-placed white light never hurt anyone.

You humans don't give fun enough attention, in my humble opinion. It's what's really important, you know.

Dogs never forget how to have fun. Just look at me! I'm ready for my treats and a long nap, but you don't see me sitting around moping because those things aren't happening. I'm paying attention to everything around me. For example, I'm just about to sink my nose into what I'm sure will be a delightful smell just beyond the length of this leash.

What's fun about that, you'd probably ask if you could hear me? Other than the smell, itself, of course. The game I'm about to play to get Mommy to let me move far enough to get to that smell. Maybe I'll pretend I'm an army dog and wiggle over to it on my belly. She never notices how far I've moved when I do that. No. That's too easy. I'm up for more of a challenge today. I think I'll use my patented Spaniel Mesmerizing Look and "convince" her to let me get to it. Or, maybe I could...

Well, you get the idea.

So, when's the last time you had fun, Mr. Doctor? Mmmmm? Really enjoy the weekly golf game, do you? I didn't think so. But I bet you'd love to get your fingers around that ball so you could throw it to me. 'Cause I know you find me really cute...an obvious point since everyone does. But you're not going to let yourself give in to the urge to play with me. Why? Because THAT WOULD BE FUN. And you just can't recognize it when it's staring you in the face. So, you lose.

Doesn't matter, really. The important thing is Larry is winning. He's beginning to remember what "happy" is, and that joy is spurring on his healing process. This afternoon, he's taken a huge step toward recovering. Now I can only hope you humans don't screw this up.

Siiiiigh. Come to think of it, maybe I'm too tired for that smell right now. I'm really ready for a treat and a nap.

Mom? My work here is done. Can we leave now?

HOMEGROWN THERAPY

Therapy work with Kalli didn't need a formal structure for marvels to occur. Our little dog brought about the wondrous all the time. Her interactions with Billy, the son of college friends I mentioned earlier, were classic examples.

Each time they were together, his hugs and kisses smothered her. To her credit, Kalli accepted the adulation with good grace. It seemed as if Billy was the exception to Kalli's rule of disdaining extreme human adoration. She appeared to sense he was very special.

As Billy aged, his sharp brain and keen sense of humor blossomed. And so did his relationship with Kalli. Their time together was always filled with laughter, balls sailing through the air, chunks of birthday cake and barbeque chicken and cookies sneaked under the dining table, a wiggling dog butt, and a little boy's face wreathed in a huge grin.

As Billy recovered from a surgical procedure one summer, Kalli spent time by his wheelchair, lavishing him with her attention. She raced through the parks around Evanston with him after he recovered. And she gracefully invited Billy to visit her when she and I took agility classes a few months after the surgery.

Held in a giant auditorium, the class boasted the very finest in jumps, tunnels, weave polls, and so forth. A white picket fence surrounded the course, and a gate by the spectator stands allowed easy access in and out of the ring. It was in these stands on that steamy

August evening that I seated nine-year-old Billy with the request that he stay put. With his Cheshire-cat grin, he agreed, and settled among the other spectators to watch the class.

Kalli was in fine fettle now that she had not only an audience, but her own private fan club watching her every move. I could tell from the spring in her step and the wide smile fixed on her face that she was having the time of her life. This was not surprising. After all, Kalli came from a long line of show dogs who lived to perform in front of a human crowd. Indeed, her father had sired more champion dogs than almost any other English cocker in history. Mugging to the masses was buried deep in Kalli's DNA.

Class began calmly enough, with Kalli obeying my agility cues to the letter. She was spectacular as she sailed over jumps, hurtled through the tunnel, danced along the dog walk, scaled the A-frame with abandon, and slammed the seesaw with a satisfying smack. Her down-stay on the table was a thing of beauty.

I should have been worried. But I was distracted by Billy's presence and lulled by Kalli's sterling performance.

The clue to impending problems rested in the fact that the equipment exercises, at which Kalli excelled during the first part of class, were set up at the opposite end of the arena from the audience stands. She never came close to Billy. But that would soon change as the exercises ended and the dogs began to work a practice course. This required the use of the entire space…including that portion of the floor running inside the fence by the spectators.

And Billy.

The handlers received the course outline and one by one, each dog/handler team ran the circuit. It was a fairly simple routine, and I'll admit to feeling smug as I snapped off Kalli's leash and positioned her in a sit-stay on the course threshold. She reinforced my good humor by giving me her undivided attention.

With a smart wave of my arm, I released Kalli and motioned to the first jump. She was picture perfect as she cleared the hurdle and moved on to the tire. Effortlessly, she jumped through its midst and we headed for the tunnel. And so it went. Pure agility heaven.

Until we reached the table. This was placed directly in front of Billy…and the gate to the audience that now stood ajar.

The first indicator that my perfect evening was about to dissolve was the fact that Kalli settled on the table in a down-stay facing Billy, rather than me. This drew a titter from the crowd as I stood by the table with Kalli's butt in my face. Muttering under my breath, I opted to walk around the table until I was at her head, rather than disrupt the command by making her move. Second indicator was Kalli's stub tail that began thumping against the table with an ever-increasing rhythm. Soon, her entire butt was gyrating, and I idly wondered how much she could move it and still be in a "stay" position.

I followed the direction of her gaze and realized that Billy's grin and waving hand were the instigators of her building frenzy.

That was when I realized I was in trouble.

I counted the seconds of Kalli's down-stay. Time was up. I barely twitched a finger to release her and Kalli was off the table like a shot. Unfortunately, she wasn't headed for the weave poles, which represented the next assigned spot in the circuit. Nope. Kalli was through the opening in the gate before I could utter a sound.

In an instant, she had flung herself onto Billy's lap with a defiant flick of her stub tail.

Laughter echoed throughout the arena, punctuated by Billy's whoops of delight. Kalli turned her head to look back at me and woofed, just to make certain I received her message.

I know, I know. I'm not supposed to be here. But, how cool is this? And everyone loves me. Look at the pure joy on every face in this audience. I've given them real pleasure, not to mention some unbeatable entertainment. Isn't that more important than coiling myself around those stupid poles like a canine snake?

I'm telling you, I'm born to entertain. Born to it. If there was an award for best dog entertainer, I'd win it right now.

What? Hmmmmm?

Oh. You're really upset with me. And embarrassed.

Come on. Even you have to find the humor in this. I'm just too damned cute for you not to get sucked into the moment.

Wait. What do I see before me? Is that the hint of a smile on those lips? Yes, it is. Admit it, you think this is funny.

And...you want me off his lap and at your feet right now.

Siiiiiiiigh. Okay, I guess I've milked the moment for as much as I can get out of it. Back to those tedious pole things.

I did my best not to laugh. God knows, I didn't want to encourage Kalli's disobedience. But really, when you have a comedian for a dog, how can you not celebrate it?

And so it was that I giggled my way through the rest of the class with my dog. Billy, of course, couldn't stop talking about the evening. He recounted the story of how she landed in his lap many times, and it soon became a staple in our repertoire of Kalli tales.

WESTWARD HO!

The first five years of Kalli's life were spent in a stable environment that comes from living in the same house, in the same community. Relationships were created and grew within this framework, whether they revolved around Carly's Group, the neighborhood, or friends made in the parks along Lake Michigan. This was about to change in the most dramatic way possible when Marc brought home news that he'd been offered a job opportunity too attractive to turn down. The vice-president of marketing slot was a dream come true for him. Unfortunately, the significant pay increase came with a hefty price tag.

The job was in Denver. And so was our new home.

Marc began his job in the fall. It wouldn't be until the next summer that we'd move, *en famille*, to Colorado. In the interim, he commuted home on the weekends, and I whirled into hyper mode preparing the house for the real estate market.

My emotions about this life change were mixed in the extreme. I was thrilled for Marc. I was furious with Marc. My strong feelings spilled over onto my dog.

I'll admit it, I was snappish and irritable. Suddenly, Kalli's obedience skills seemed sloppy to me. She was too slow to drop into a down-stay, too fast taking treats from my hand, too imprecise as she walked around me in a by-heel finish.

And I was so distracted, I didn't pay attention to her raised-eyebrow expressions of annoyance. I didn't heed them as the early-warning signals they were. Finally, when my never-suffer-fools dog started growling at me, ever so softly, I began to take note of her.

You really need to take a chill pill, Mom. I get it. You hate the idea of leaving this house and moving away to something named Colorado. (Yes, I know all about it. You see, I listen carefully when you and Daddy talk to each other. I pick up all sorts of useful information that way. After all, knowledge is power.)

And yeah, I understand that, for once, it's not all about you. But that's the way it goes. Hey, I'm affected by this, too. You know how into my routine I am. I'll miss my favorite sniffing places along the lakefront and barking at that annoying beagle down the street. I'll even miss the girls downtown. But, it's not all about me, either.

So, you made your decision to support Daddy. Now, you have to follow through and do it. No more of the pain-in-the-ass drama queen routine. Okay? Remember, this career thingie is huge for him.

I suggest you suck it up and get on with what you have to do. This place isn't going to sell itself, you know.

Poor Kalli had her work cut out for her as she dealt with me during this transition period. Home improvement projects meant once-cozy living spaces were ripped to shreds and uninhabitable for long stretches of time. At one point in early winter, the handyman we'd hired demolished a wall in the living room to reveal a stained glass window a previous owner had dry-walled over for some inexplicable reason. Dust and grime coated every surface. I found the conditions unbearable and launched into a temper tantrum of which I'm not terribly proud.

Right around that time, Kalli began licking her right front paw. It was obsessive behavior. After the fact, I realized she used the licking action as a tranquilizer, a way to calm herself in the face of my manic activity and the upheaval that now characterized her home.

At the time, deep in a narcissistic pit, I acknowledged her situation through a haze of annoyance. It was one more thing for me to deal with. Still, I managed to shrug off my self-absorption and scheduled a vet appointment. After a thorough checkup, Kalli was sent home with antiseptic salve and a bandaged paw.

We entered the kitchen, and I glanced down to see her standing before me with her "bad" paw raised off the floor and a pathetic "poor me" expression in her deep brown eyes. In spite of myself, I burst out laughing. "Milking it for all it's worth, are you? And Alpha Dad isn't even home to appreciate this."

With her characteristic *Humph,* she turned her back on me and settled on the living room couch. Within minutes, she was snoring.

I left her and drove to a nearby Target store for baby socks. We would place them on her paw once the vet's bandage disappeared…anything to keep her healing pads from growing raw once more.

I purchased a large collection of socks in an array of sizes and colors, and hightailed it home. It turned out Kalli was a perfect fit for the preemie size. Soon, she raced through her days swathed in pale pink socks with yellow ruffles, blue polka dots fringed with pink lace, and pistachio green stripes studded with white hearts.

She seemed proud of her adornment and promptly stopped licking. After all, not only did she attract attention on her walks because of her inherent good looks, but now she plucked her public's heart strings—she was "injured" *and*

wearing baby socks. How much more appealing could she possibly get?

"That dog should act in soap operas," Marc said the following Saturday morning during our walk. "Talk about manipulating people's emotions!"

We had just left a group of Northwestern coeds as they oohed and aahed over Kalli. One of them had actually picked up her pink-stripe-bedecked paw and kissed it.

Kalli had deigned to remain still long enough to receive their adoration. She looked up at the girls through thick eyelashes, her studied "sad little me" expression tinged with satisfaction. A smug smile flashed across her muzzle. More fans had been reeled in. Life didn't get any better for Kalli.

Of course, she'd felt the need to admonish one young woman. Too much adoration repelled Kalli, after all. When the giggling and head-stroking had continued a bit too long, Kalli had withdrawn her paw from the coed's hand, *humphed*, and literally shook off the girl, leaving the blonde standing on the path, mouth agape, staring after her.

"You really are a shit," I told the top of Kalli's head as she strolled beside me.

She glanced up at me and winked. "Really a shit," I repeated under my breath.

Well, of course I am. But I brushed off that girl for a very good reason. What kind of life do you think she'll have if she loses control like that at every turn? You might not have been aware of it, but her feelings were too strong. They were...how do you say it? Oh, yes. Out of proportion for the situation.

And, um, as long as we're on the subject of feelings getting the better of humans, do you see a similarity between this girl's over-emotional state and yours, Mom? Mmmmmm? You really should, you know. If you're paying the slightest bit of attention.

I'm tired of seeing you lose it as we get ready to move. I thought we'd discussed this already, and how we need to get over ourselves so we can support Daddy.

You need to learn how to accept stuff. To just let things flow. But instead, you get all bent out of shape and fight for control. Now, there's nothing wrong with control. I'm a master at it, as you well know. But sometimes you have to figure out when to let go. And that's exactly the deal now.

We're going to Colorado, and that's all there is to it. Stop fighting it. That's just a stupid waste of time and energy. And stop getting me involved in your mess. Remember, I'm honor-bound to help you process all the negative crap. And there's been a ton of it lately. No wonder I was chewing my paws.

Christmas approached. Marc and I received an invitation to the annual holiday party hosted by his new employer. It was black-tie formal. I found the necessity to pull together an evening ensemble for the event frustrating. And the ensuing trip seemed downright formidable to me—it signaled my first foray into Colorado.

After settling Kalli at Kristen's, I hopped on a plane and joined Marc at the residential hotel he was calling home in the Mile High City. Once social obligations ended and the party had come and gone, we joined a Realtor friend-of-a-friend and began looking at houses. My goal was to find suitable property quickly. The last thing I wanted to do was prolong the wrenching process of leaving Chicago and finding new digs in Colorado.

Marc and I spent the next few days wandering through houses on the real estate market. Nothing interested us. We admitted defeat and called a halt to our search, reconciling ourselves to the prospect of future house-hunting junkets. Just as our Realtor swung his car around to begin the downhill trek to Denver, I noticed a "mountain contemporary" with a "For Sale" sign out front.

"What about this one?" I nodded toward the rambling wooden structure, noting its warm brown stain and cheerful blue trim. It was nestled into a hillside, the land sweeping down from the front entrance, and was surrounded by a Ponderosa pine forest. Set in the heart of the Rocky Mountain foothills, it was forty minutes southwest of downtown Denver.

Marc stared at it for a long moment. "Isn't it a bit...big...for us?"

"Probably. But most of the smaller houses up here are mountain cabins I don't really like."

"Yeah, you're right. The nicer properties have been on the large side. We may have to buy bigger to get the features we want."

"Exactly. Let's check out this place, at least. I mean, we're here. And we have a bit of time before I absolutely must leave for the airport."

Within minutes, we'd entered the empty house. I breathed a sigh of relief as I glanced around me. The place consisted of three levels and was large for just the two of us...er, *three* of us. But it was otherwise acceptable.

I appreciated the soaring, window-studded, two-story entrance, and the wide stairway leading up to its three bedrooms. On the upper floor, I noticed the guest bath was significantly larger than the one-and-only tiny bathroom in our Evanston home.

After passing two bedrooms—each spacious and airy—I walked into the master suite at the end of the hall. An open doorway in a back corner of the suite beckoned, and I entered the master bathroom.

I burst out laughing as my eyes swept across the Palladian window over the jetted tub nestled in a bay, the tumbled stone shower stall, and tiled double-sink counter. The space was almost as large as our bedroom in Evanston. Perhaps coming to Colorado had its perks.

The five-year-old house boasted other attributes as well, including three fireplaces. One of these was set in a massive rock column at one end of a family room adjacent to the kitchen and breakfast nook. Patio doors led from the room onto a deck surrounded by pine trees.

We descended stairs to the lower level of the house, which was described as a "walk-out." This meant what would normally be a subterranean basement was partially above ground, thanks to the angle of the sloping land. An expansive deck ran the entire length of the structure at this lower level. Beautiful big windows looked out onto a wooded backyard with a sports court in a far corner. One end of the lower level boasted patio doors leading to the deck.

As was always the case whenever I'd assessed real estate property in the past, the selling feature for me was the spot I picked to become my office. Immediately, I saw my desk set in the heart of the house's lower level, facing those patio doors. And I saw the doors open, with Kalli bouncing in and out of the house at will. A perfect work space for human and dog. I'd found our Colorado home.

Marc didn't need much convincing. He didn't want to spend time shopping, either. We assembled an offer to purchase the property immediately.

My good humor over the transaction dampened when I swung by to pick up Kalli from Kristen's upon my return to Chicago. I sensed something wrong the moment I parked the car and walked up the path to her front door. I'd seen Kalli playing in the side yard with a mix of Kristen's own dogs and the latest in an ever-changing group of board-and-train clients. While the dogs had been romping, there had been a noticeable lack of *joie de vivre* that was the usual mood in the roomy yard. When Kristen responded to my knock and I saw the drawn look on her normally vibrant face, I knew something had happened.

She hugged me, then left to fetch Kalli. My dog entered the room in a distracted sort of way…completely atypical, especially since I'd been gone for a few days. Normally, she'd race to my side with a madly wriggling butt and demand I spend the next two days constantly petting her, as if I needed a remedial course in how to do it. This time, she approached me and deigned to allow me to pat her head, then left me to settle by Kristen's side.

I looked at my friend, one eyebrow cocked in a silent question.

"She's just fulfilling her role as therapy dog, Laura."

"What happened?" I could feel a slimy cold settle in my stomach.

"Darcy passed away two days ago."

I stared at her in disbelief. Kristen's Lab, Darcy, was only five years old. The dog had never been sick a day in her life. Indeed, she'd had a litter of puppies six months earlier, and had breezed through the delivery and care of the puppies as if they were the easiest things in the world.

"Stomach bloat," Kristen continued in a deadened voice. "It happened too fast. We couldn't get her to the vet in time to save her."

Stomach bloat is indeed a dreaded condition, known to be fatal if not attended to immediately. It's often caused by the animal swallowing air. The stomach swells in response, which may lead to the organ twisting, trapping air, food, and water. The bloated stomach obstructs veins in the abdomen, leading to low blood pressure, shock, and damage to internal organs. The combined effect can kill a dog in a flash. Not even the most seasoned owner like Kristen can do anything if the condition comes on quickly.

I wrapped her in my arms and hugged her. Visions of Darcy going about her animal-assisted therapy work swept through my mind. The affable Lab had been sweet, gentle, and exquisitely trained. Therapy clients had loved her. And she'd been the perfect foil for my frenetic spaniel.

Kristen shuddered in my embrace and pulled back to drop into her chair once again. Kalli pressed against her leg.

group identified as "DenverDogs." Perfect. I joined and had introduced myself to the group within five minutes, explaining to the members I was relocating to the area with an English cocker and was eager to launch new doggie activities.

I received hearty notes of welcome from many of the members, and a personal email from one woman. Dina Smith had just moved into the Denver area, herself, and was already deeply involved in agility work with her Australian shepherds. She'd noticed my description of Kalli's agility background and invited me to meet her and her dogs once we'd settled in our Colorado home. She had friends who owned English cockers and had grown to love the breed. She was eager to get to know Kalli and her humans.

This connection eased the transition as we prepared to move across country. Knowing we had a new friend waiting for us comforted me.

As packing crews descended upon the house with piles of boxes, rolls of packing paper, and giant cubes of bubble wrap, I got Kalli out of there. No reason to subject her to the craziness and chaos. We left her with Kristen.

The end of May saw us waving farewell to the bulging moving van as it pulled away from the curb and began its trek to Colorado. I resolutely ignored the emptiness of the house around us. We walked out the door, our steps echoing in the void, and left to pick up Kalli at Kristen's house. Numbed by the magnitude of the changes in my life, I never felt Kristen's arms around me as she gave me a huge hug.

Kalli bounced up and down at my feet. She was ready to leave. She was ready for an adventure.

I shook my head at her. "How do you do that? Turn every moment into delight? Even the tough ones, for God's sake!"

I'm simply enjoying myself. Challenges are fun, Mom. They're not the tragedies you try to make them.

Oh, don't give me that hurt, human look. You're reeking with that victim thing you do.

You have a choice. Choose fun! That's the spaniel way.

We spent our first night on the road in a Nebraska motel that was doggie friendly. Not only did the motel owner allow pets to stay in the rooms with their humans, he had set up a gorgeous, enclosed play yard for visiting canines. Of course, Kalli was bored with the yard after ten minutes of exploring its various scents. With a collective sigh, Marc and I hooked her up to a leash and took off down the road, knowing it was going to take far more than an enclosed space to exercise and entertain her.

"Why can't you be like other dogs?" I asked her as we returned from our hour-long walk down the suburban streets surrounding the motel. "I mean, most dogs would be more than happy to chase a few balls in the fenced-in area and be done with the exercise portion of their day."

"Why do you waste your energy asking?" Marc rejoined. "After all this time, surely you must have realized Kalli is unlike any other dog we've ever seen."

I looked down at my spaniel and met her wide, unblinking brown stare. I could have sworn she was laughing at me.

After a second day of driving and yet another doggie-friendly hotel that welcomed Kalli with open arms, noon on the third day saw us pulling into the driveway of our new home. We'd arrived a full day before the moving van was scheduled to reach us, so for the moment, we had a rambling, very empty house to fill with nothing but ourselves.

Kalli was ecstatic. She raced from room to room, enjoying the traction of our newly installed carpeting, unhampered by such pesky things as furniture. She careened onto the decks, tore down the hill to the tennis court behind the house and bounded back up the hill to the deck. She was on her way down the hill a second time—steep hillsides were new experiences for her—when she froze in place.

Sitting on the lower level deck with a book in my hand, I looked up at the unexpected silence. Trotting across the overgrown grass between the house and the court was a black fox. Did this wild beast present a danger to Kalli? How would my dog, who shunned other canines like the plague and far and away preferred human company to any animal, react to our unexpected visitor?

I left my book and walked down the steps from the deck into the yard. As I approached the pair, I yearned for a camera. (Why did I never have one when I really wanted one?) The fox had slowed its trot to calm steps and then halted. The two animals faced each other four feet apart. Suddenly, the fox dropped into a play bow before Kalli.

A play bow? It couldn't be. And yet, it must have communicated to Kalli in that universal language only canines can understand, because Kalli answered it with a bow of her own, then charged.

The fox leapt straight into the air, spun, and took off toward the meadow next to the house. The move was pure cartoon roadrunner. Then, a sound came to my ears I hadn't heard very much in the last few months: my own laughter. With it came release. Emotional tension and pain that had gripped me since I'd first learned we were moving to Colorado began to drain away.

I took a deep breath and smiled. Leave it to Kalli—and her new friend—to find a way to relax the grip of trauma I'd allowed to assume way too much importance in my life. And with that breath came a reminder that I really needed to retrieve my dog. Because she was gone.

Oh, not gone—gone. I could see her bounding over the rolling ground in the meadow, but she was racing in the opposite direction from me, and I had no idea how far away she'd run. The good news was the fox was nowhere to be seen. Clearly, the little athlete had outpaced my dog. Which meant Kalli would soon grow bored and return on her own.

Sure enough, within a minute, she appeared, her black-and-white face grinning, her black ears flowing through the air as she climbed the side of a small ravine that separated the house from the meadow. She flung herself at me, a happy spaniel with wagging tail.

"Just a bit different from what you're used to, huh? Welcome to Colorado, Kalli."

I think it's going to be okay, Mom. That black thing was really cute. We didn't have those back at...the other place. And you know what's really, really cool? The windows in the house. Did you know they go all the way to the floor?

Oh, yeah, I guess you do. But, from my perspective, that's the best thing ever. Because I can see outside any time I want to. From all over the place. I can even lie down and still see outside.

That's a big change, and I must say, it's about time. I think back to my perch on the front stairs in the hallway of that other house and I feel downright sorry for myself. That was the only way I could see the yard and street, for pity's sake!

And let me tell you, there's lots to look at here. I'm expecting all sorts of animals to show up in our yard. Because I can smell them. I'm not sure what they're going to look like, but I know it's going to be lots of fun. Especially if you let me chase them. And when that black thing shows up to play again, I'll know it right away.

So cool.

The fox was just the first visitor Kalli encountered on our property. Over the years, she went nose-to-nose with coyote, white-tail deer, mule deer—even a flock of wild turkeys. Thankfully, she was safely tucked in the house when the mountain lion appeared in our meadow at dusk later that summer.

One of the most notable animals to visit us showed up when we'd lived in the house only a few weeks. Our first clue to his appearance was a frenetic spaniel tearing from one end of the house to the other, barking her head off. It was the Kalli alert we'd learned to take seriously.

From the corner of my eye, I saw movement on the deck outside our family room in the gathering gloom of an early evening. And there, in the center of the space, a hummingbird feeder cupped in one paw, was a giant black bear staring at us through the glass of our patio door.

By this point, Kalli had spotted him, too, and she was lunging at the door. I snapped a leash on her and pulled her back to me, keeping her secure by my side as the man of the house headed for the kitchen.

"Um, Marc? The bear's out there," I yelled over Kalli's snarling.

"Yup. He'll be gone in no time." Emerging from the kitchen with a stainless steel tablespoon and a metal pot, Marc grinned at me and headed for the deck. "It's all about noise. A bit of banging and he'll be gone in an instant." Vaguely, I wondered how he'd known that.

By this point, the bear had consumed the sugar water and flung the feeder to the deck floor. Now, he was standing by the glass door, looking into the house with what I swear was a grin on his face.

"What? You've had your sugar water appetizer and now you're waiting for the main course?" I asked him.

Kalli's snarling grew louder. I looked down at her. "Nope. You're not going out there, kid. I doubt you'd be that tasty after hummingbird water, but I'm betting he'd still attack you, if for no other reason than to shut you up."

Marc paused in front of the patio door. "Just take a look at that guy, will you? He's magnificent."

As Marc had gotten closer to him, the bear had started backing his way to the tree he'd climbed to get on the deck in the first place. Now, he swung onto a branch, his eyes still on the approaching human.

Marc opened the patio door a crack and banged the pot.

I winced at the racket. I wasn't sure the bear would run at the sound, but I certainly wanted to.

Sure enough, the bear had had enough of us for one evening. He dropped to the ground and lumbered through the yard. We scrambled out onto the deck in time to see his dark form swallowed by shadows in the far corner of our pine forest.

While Kalli hadn't gotten up close and personal with the bear, that wasn't the case with another guest who showed up in our backyard months later. A herd of elk had been grazing on the lush grass that surrounded our sports court…not an unusual event. Kalli and I had been watching them from the lower level deck. While I kept a close eye on my dog, I knew she'd been around enough elk in recent weeks to have grown used to them.

Yeah, they're really boring. I mean, they're big and look like they could be really scary, but they aren't. They just hang out and eat the grass. They need to get a life.

But, wait a minute. Look at that, Mom. That thing that just jumped our fence is even bigger than they are, with pointy things sticking out of his head. He looks a lot more interesting than those others. I have to check this out.

I watched Kalli climb down the steps to the yard without thinking about it. The females had migrated to a far corner, and I assumed Kalli was going to investigate the smells they'd left behind as she normally did. Then, something made me take a closer look. Stepping out from a clump of scrub oak was a giant, majestic bull elk.

He wasn't amused with my little dog.

Kalli wasn't helping matters as she barked her head off at him, standing her ground.

The elk took a few steps toward her. She responded with a few steps of her own, edging ever closer to him.

Suddenly, the beast lowered his head in Kalli's direction, the spikes of his impressive rack of antlers piercing the air, aimed right at her.

Alarm bolted through me as I realized he was getting ready to charge her. Meanwhile, oblivious to the target painted on her back, Kalli pranced around him, bouncing on her front legs, the perfect picture of an officious watchdog.

My heart in my mouth, I called out, "Kalli, come!" Amazing how calm I could sound in an emergency. Because I knew if there were ever a time when Kalli needed to respond to a recall, it was right there and then.

She hesitated a second, looked from the elk to me, then turned in my direction and trotted to me after giving the elk one last woof. She arrived at my side with a self-satisfied grin.

"Good girl." I barely recognized my quivering voice. So much for being calm. But the image of my black-and-white baby gored by that giant had taken hold, and I couldn't get it out of my head.

For his part, the bull elk glared at us for a long moment, then led his ladies out of our yard.

From that point on, Kalli and I showed major respect for the elk and gave them wide berth—whether male or female.

A NEW WORLD

As we settled into our new life tucked into the "first fold of the Rockies," far more than the wildlife marked the dramatic contrast from the Chicago we'd known so well. Still, I did my best to reproduce old patterns.

We adhered to the traditional hour-long walking event in the middle of the day, but gone were the groomed urban parks of Evanston. Now, we confronted dirt paths winding through mountainsides of Ponderosa pines and aspens. I couldn't even call the event a "walk" any longer. What Kalli and I did each day could only be described as a "hike."

Our first outing took place in an area known as an "Open Space Park," managed by the county in which we lived. The land had been part of a famous cattle and horse ranch at one time. While descendants of the original pioneering family still lived in the historic Victorian house adjacent to the park, they had donated their acreage to the county in an effort to preserve it. It was famous for its walking trails meandering across meadows, up and down hillsides, through dense stands of pine trees, and over seasonal creeks.

Kalli bounded out of the car in the parking lot, eager to explore. Nose to ground, she made it as far as the edge of the lot before she became mesmerized by the scents emanating from boulders that rimmed the area. I'm guessing every dog visiting the park used those boulders as receptacles for their calling cards. Kalli's nose stuck to the rocky surfaces as her nostrils inhaled each smelly nuance.

I gave her some time to work the area while I watched parties of hikers follow the winding path beyond the parking lot. I looked down at Kalli. She had no interest in moving beyond the boulders. Indeed, I recognized the body language as she settled in for a long stint of tracking and sniffing, all within a few feet of the car.

"Uh, Kalli?"

No response. Her black nose swept the craggy edge of the next boulder in line.

"Okay, little girl. Here's the deal. We're here to *walk*. You know, exercise? Look at the beautiful woods over there." I swept an arm toward the trees. No response from the spaniel.

I started to pull her away from the rocks, then stopped myself. I could remember many instances in Chicago when Kalli had focused on a limited area, and I'd let her do her thing for long minutes. Yet here I was eager to move on, to get into the woods and walk the trails.

I glanced around me, seeing pine-studded hills crown the skyline, sculpting a scalloped green crest that disappeared into the distant bluish haze. Spreading away from the parking lot and surrounding the rambling hiking trail was a meadow brimming with wildflowers. Fuchsia and pink daisy-like heads bobbed in the breeze. Blue and yellow spikes jutted from the grasses, an exclamation point demanding attention. The little girl inside me wanted to rush into their midst and flop down, burying my head in their fragrance.

Indeed, the setting was spectacular wherever I looked. Somehow, spending time on the edge of a gritty, heat-packed parking lot seemed almost…sacrilegious.

Oh, please, Mom. Aren't you taking this beautiful landscape scenic thing a bit too far? I mean, I suppose it's pretty enough. But it sure doesn't compare to the scents I'm picking up from these rocks. These Colorado dogs are a wild bunch, I'm telling you.

Hmmmmm? You're really serious about moving on? Oh, man. I don't see the attraction over there. It's just a bunch of trees. I don't even see any lawn to run across. And there's no sidewalk! How can we expect to take a walk without pavement? Oh, and do I need to point out there's not a squirrel in sight? No, wait a moment. There's one over by those trees. But geesh! That can hardly be called a regular squirrel, can it? I mean, it looks nothing like the ones I'm used to. These things are so...so...primitive. I bet they don't understand the tracking game. At least I was able to train a few to play along with me next to the lakefront in Evanston.

But, I digress. Look, give me five more minutes to sniff, then I promise I'll be on my best spaniel behavior when we trudge through those ugly trees over there.

"Sorry, Kalli. But we're going for a walk. It's time to explore."

To her credit, my little dog responded to my words almost immediately. I unhooked the leash to sweeten the pot. I'd looked around us and hadn't seen a dog or human for the last few minutes, so decided to take the gamble and risk a ticket in order to let Kalli have the freedom she relished. Waving my arm, I called to her and we set off, following the trail as it dropped into the heart of the meadow.

Thus began a pattern of reluctant cooperation on the part of the spaniel during our Colorado walks. Oh, she hiked the trails with us readily enough, but never with the zeal she'd exhibited tracking squirrels in the urban parks of the Chicago area. Indeed, as she grew older, she became so bored with our outings, we kept her on command for the first part of the hike to make certain she'd go the distance. The return trip always passed in a blur, Kalli picking up steam the closer she got to the car.

In short, the breathtakingly beautiful trails found throughout the rich array of open space parks around our home engendered the same condescending attitude from our spaniel as had the doggie play groups earlier in her life. Occasionally, the trails became downright uncomfortable for her. Like the time we were following a narrow path that was part of an expansive public land area winding above Indian Hills and Kittredge, two mountain towns within ten minutes' drive of our house.

As we made our way along the side of a mountain, I watched my footing carefully. A steep drop-off immediately next to the path had earned my respect. Kalli sailed forward, unconcerned about hazardous rocks and possible falls, her paws striking a solid rhythm on the dry, packed surface.

We rounded a sharp curve in the trail and discovered that a party of horses and their riders was coming toward us.

Now, Kalli had never seen a horse before she landed in Colorado. Marc and I had been trying to acclimate her to them, using a neighbor's friendly horses as her teachers. Every day, we'd walk past their pasture. Most of the time, the pair had been turned out to graze and would immediately gravitate toward us as soon as they spotted us. The gentle giants were accustomed to dogs, living with a pair of Labs, and thus had neither shyness nor nervousness around Kalli.

For her part, Kalli was wary and highly curious. She'd approach them on tense, stiff legs primed to carry her to safety at the first suspicious twitch of an equine ear.

Initially, their every movement caused her to bolt. But gradually, Kalli's native intelligence kicked in and she realized the animals were harmless.

Well, geesh. Who can blame me for being a bit uncertain around them? Look at those ugly big things. Have you ever seen anything so ungainly? How was I to know they wouldn't hurt me?

And frankly, Mom, now that I'm more used to them, I must say, they aren't the brightest bulbs, are they? And what are they good for? They can't retrieve game birds in a field, or race around a line of weave poles, or sail over an agility jump.

Mmmm? What's that? They do jump? With people on their backs?

Now, you're making no sense whatsoever. Why on earth would they go over agility jumps with humans riding them? Mmmm? They're used for transportation sometimes? Why? Don't people have cars or bikes?

This is just silly. I don't get the attraction humans have for them. I tell you, they just aren't good for anything.

I was thankful for Kalli's exposure to our equine neighbors as I watched the four horses approach us. But while I was reasonably comfortable Kalli wouldn't panic at their proximity, I wasn't sure how we'd engineer logistics so the horse party could pass us on that narrow trail. There didn't seem to be room for all of us. I looked around frantically and noticed that the hillside flattened just a bit a few yards ahead.

I hurried to the spot, then scooped Kalli into my arms. I held her close to me, praying there was enough clearance for the horses if I plastered her flat against my chest.

Kalli was never crazy about being picked up and carried. Usually she tolerated it, but never let an episode pass without theatrical groans and moans, signaling her martyred attitude toward a situation in which her humans had their way without giving her a voice in the matter.

This time was no different, and she grunted her displeasure as we waited for the riding party to reach our spot on the path. Her vocalizations ceased abruptly when she realized the giants were coming right at her. She couldn't get close enough to me as the first horse passed by.

Its rider—a woman about my age—smiled down at us. "Oh, what a darling! What kind of dog is that?"

"That's an English cocker, Marjorie," chimed the rider second in line. "And a beauty at that."

Two horses had safely passed us, and Kalli must have noticed she was still alive to tell the tale.

When the third horse approached, it slowed until it stood next to us. Then, it gently stretched its head toward her and slurped at Kalli's muzzle with its long tongue.

Its rider giggled. "I'm so sorry, but Patchwork just loves dogs. She can't let an opportunity pass to give kisses."

The horse hovered for a minute longer, nuzzling Kalli until my dog began to struggle in my arms. Then its rider urged the animal on.

When the last horse had passed us, its rider nodding her thanks, I eased Kalli to the ground and laughed aloud. My little dog was the picture of righteous indignation. She had braced her four legs, paws dug into the dirt, head raised as she glared at the horses in the distance.

Oh...my...God!

It wasn't bad enough that those mangy things came that close to me, but to give me a kiss? Yuck! I'm going to die of giant animal disease. I mean, that monster has to be loaded with germs.

Mom? This isn't funny. Not one bit.

You know, I'm not at all sure about this Colorado place. I never had anything like this happen to me in Chicago!

Well, at least take me home and give me a very long bath.

While Colorado outings might not have compared to squirrel tracking in Evanston parks, they weren't a total bore for my spaniel, either. One of Kalli's favorite recreational events during snowy weather was to hang out near the sledding hill of a nearby open space park.

Gentle, sloping terrain extended from the fringe of heavy forests and stretched through the heart of a giant meadow at the edge of the park. Safely tucked away from roadways, it was the perfect place for little ones—and not so little ones—to enjoy the snow on a variety of devices. Everything from saucers and air boards to high-tech toboggans and not-so-high-tech tubes whooshed across the meadow. Shouts of joy, laughter, and good-natured screams sliced through the frosty air on any day that saw snow on the ground.

But a major attraction of the meadow had nothing to do with the white stuff. Rather, it revolved around a little white-and-black number who stole the show as soon as she arrived on the scene.

We quickly picked up on the symbiotic relationship between the kids and Kalli. And of course, our dog did everything she could to weight the balance toward her end of the equation.

She'd eye the kids the moment she descended from the car. Then, she'd saunter across the parking lot and begin her nonchalant trot through the meadow. She calculated exactly where to position herself to maximize her exposure to the children. Once she'd selected a spot, she merely had to sit in place for a short time in order to be noticed.

And noticed she was. The tiny snow athletes nearest Kalli would begin to bug their parents to let them go over to "pet the doggie."

Then Kalli would tilt her face to the most endearing angle, designed to hook the parents, who would want to come over to pet her, too.

Once this first group had surrounded her, others noticed the activity swirling around the spaniel and joined the fun. Soon, Kalli was holding court, and sledding gear of all shapes and sizes lay strewn across the icy meadow, forgotten.

As always, Kalli demanded dignity among her audience. Those who knew her well could identify the revulsion creeping across her face as poor unfortunates crossed her imaginary line of civility. But she was never rude, even with the misguided. And usually she accepted the compliments and strokes of admiration with the calm that characterized her approach to the world. It was her due, this fawning attention, and she accepted it as such.

When she grew weary of her impromptu fan club, Kalli rose and strolled through the crowd with the imperial dignity of a monarch reviewing her loyal subjects. The horde would clear before Her Majesty, the Queen. Then, after dropping onto the back seat of our SUV, she'd heave a sigh of contentment and fall fast asleep.

Another aspect of Kalli's life that changed in Colorado was her attitude toward squirrels and birds.

When we first moved to Colorado, Marc and I had decided to put up bird feeders in the yard, not to attract our feathered friends, but to draw the squirrels. (Although we quickly grew to love the birds and continued to fill each feeder to the brim every day we lived in the house.) We figured with an enclosed yard of nearly an acre, Kalli would be able to track and chase the little furry mammals to her heart's content. But her reaction to the small guys was completely different than it had been in her former yard. Here, she ignored them. It was as if they didn't exist in her world.

"Do you suppose Colorado squirrels smell differently to Kalli than those in Evanston did?" Marc asked me one night. We were sitting on the lower-level deck and watched as Kalli lay in quiet repose while a squirrel pranced in front of her, chattering nervously.

"I don't have a clue. I've gotta say, I never expected this." I nodded toward Kalli, who had closed her eyes and dropped into a doze as the squirrel munched on a peanut a few feet away from her front paws.

The squirrel seemed confused, too, dipping its head behind the peanut it held, then peeking over the top of it to stare at Kalli.

What? Oh, I know. You think I should chase that stupid rodent thing through the yard. Nah. Not here.

Dad, you were almost right when you wondered if these squirrels have a different scent than Chicago squirrels. While they do, that's not why I'm ignoring them. They're just...so...so stupid here. They're not worth my attention. Something about being out in the middle of nowhere means these things don't know how to hustle. They don't reason things out. I mean, look at the pathetic creature eating its nut right in front of me. If I'd been back home in Evanston, that squirrel would have taunted me, teased me, played a game with me. I might even have been induced to move.

City squirrels are bright and quick. They have to think through every angle just to survive. That makes them worth tracking and chasing. At least they offer a brilliant being such as me the teensiest bit of a challenge. And I appreciate that. In fact, I even respect it, which is saying quite a lot!

Yaaaaaawn. I've already wasted too much energy on this boring topic. It's time I started a serious nap.

Our theory about Kalli's change in attitude toward birds was borne out a few weeks later. The three of us were walking around the outside of the house with a contractor we had hired to power wash and stain the structure. Caught up in a conversation with the man, neither

Marc nor I were paying much attention to Kalli as she raced through the yard.

At one point, the contractor glanced down at Kalli, who was now standing next to me. His face took on an odd expression. "Ah, you might want to check out your dog."

"Excuse me?"

"I'm pretty sure she has a bird in her mouth."

"Huh?" It's times like this when my sophisticated communication skills really pay off.

Marc and I stared at Kalli. She looked up at us, the picture of innocence, not moving a muscle.

"Oh, no, you must be mistak—"

Kalli's muzzle twitched. It was a subtle gesture. I doubt if anyone but a hypersensitive doggie mom would have noticed it.

"Ummm. Kalli?" I continued my scrutiny.

Her expression was too pure…too…studied.

I knelt next to her. She turned away from me just a hair.

Then I knew something was up. With practiced efficiency, I pried open her mouth. A feathery blur flew out from between her teeth and disappeared into the sky.

"That little bugger," Marc breathed. "How did she get the whole bird into her mouth?"

"Oh, gun dogs are good at that," said the contractor with assurance.

Marc and I both turned to him. Kalli had flopped down at my feet with a disgruntled sigh.

"She has an excellent mouth," the guy went on. "Very soft. I'd love to have her out in the field with me and my buddies. She'd make a great retriever."

Kalli's head popped up, a satisfied grin spreading across her face.

"At least she didn't hurt it," Marc murmured.

"That one, she didn't," I added.

He looked at me with a silent question.

I shrugged. "You really think she would have let it go if we hadn't intervened? Her retrieving instincts only go so far, I suspect."

My memory flashed to images of Kalli sitting on our patio in Evanston, not moving a muscle as sparrows hopped across her paws. What had happened to our gentle dog?

From that point on, I kept a closer eye on Kalli when we were outside. When the occasional bird flew into one of our windows and dropped to the ground, stunned, I raced her to the impaired creature. If Kalli reached the bird first, she'd pop it into her mouth...or, as much of it as would fit in her mouth. Immediately, I'd release the prisoner. Thank God, they were always able to fly away.

I never saw Kalli kill a bird. We'll just leave it at that.

CONNECTIONS

Kalli always proved to be the instigator of new friendships—human and canine—for the entire family. Her role as diplomat and emissary of the Abbott household was especially appreciated once we'd moved to Colorado. After all, we didn't know a soul in our new area…with one exception, thanks to Kalli. I'd already made the acquaintance of Dina Smith on the DenverDogs email list while I was still in Chicago. As soon as we'd settled into our Colorado home, I looked her up.

I remembered her description of her agility work. It turned out she had set up a practice ring in her backyard and offered classes. Considering how much Kalli had always enjoyed agility, I realized this activity would provide the perfect vehicle for Marc, me, and my little dog to meet the folks around our new home. I called Dina to reserve a spot in her upcoming session.

"Mountain Agility" was a huge departure from the controlled environment of the indoor arena where we'd taken agility classes in Chicago. And Kalli didn't have a clue what to make of it. Being a creature of habit, she was accustomed to tackling the equipment on a gym floor. Combining the rolling, uneven landscape of the Denver foothills with jumps, A-frames, and weave poles didn't compute in her brain.

Well, I'm sorry, but the ground is wavy. And besides which, we're outside. How can you expect me to tear around when I don't have a wood

She looked down at my little dog with a sad smile. "She's been glued to me ever since it happened. I have to tell you, Laura, none of the others honed into the situation as quickly as Kalli did. And when they realized what was going on, she had already claimed her place by my side. The rest honored it."

Tears filled her eyes. "You can't have as many dogs as I've had over the years and not come to accept their passing. But this…" She took a trembling breath. "This came out of nowhere. One minute Darcy was fine; the next, she was gone. Even our vet was stunned with the suddenness of it all."

Kristen grabbed a tissue from a nearly empty box at her elbow and wiped her eyes. "Kalli has been the perfect comfort…not too soft or affectionate, nor too distant." Kristen laughed weakly. "I'm really going to miss her."

"Well, we haven't left yet. Haven't even gotten our place on the market." I made a quick decision not to tell Kristen about the house for which we'd just signed a sales contract.

As fate would have it, our Evanston home sold within a few weeks after it hit the market. Closing dates were set. So was our future course.

During the lull between the house sale and moving into our Colorado home, I began to search for ways to ease our transition to an area with which we were completely unfamiliar. Doggie venues seemed to be a logical place to start. After all, we were ending numerous Kalli-centric activities in the Chicago area. Replacing them in Colorado made perfect sense to me. And I felt certain that, as always, Kalli would lead us to a wide range of social connections.

Remembering the online resource network I'd hooked into when I hunted for dog breeders before I'd found Kalli, I chose to start my research on the Internet. Immediately, I found a discussion email *floor? I mean, a dog has to have standards, after all. Speaking of which, haven't you noticed it gets downright hot out here? And you know how I feel about heat. I really must have air conditioning if you want me to perform at my peak.*

I don't know about this Colorado place sometimes. Things just seem too wild here.

Eventually, Kalli did get the hang of the outdoor agility course, and classes went well for a few months. Until she started limping.

Now, other than having an irritated paw once or twice, Kalli had always been the picture of perfect health. And at five years of age, she was in the prime of her life. So when I noticed she was favoring her right front leg, I did what any self-respecting, obsessive dog mom would do.

I freaked out.

Then I called the vet and scheduled an appointment.

"Hmmm," Terri murmured as she placed Kalli on the examining table and lifted one leg, then the other.

"Hmmm, what?" I stared at our vet, silently begging her for an explanation for Kalli's limp.

Finally, she looked up at me. "Well, I don't think it's anything serious." She laughed as Kalli planted a slurp solidly on the bridge of her nose. "And I'd say our girl isn't in any significant pain." Kalli responded with a furious butt wiggle, then gently bounced on her front legs as she anticipated a treat from the kindhearted woman.

Terri had instituted the "cookie hunt" game with Kalli, and my food-crazed dog couldn't get enough of it. To prevent her from inhaling whole biscuits, Terri broke up the goodies into little morsels and dropped them on the floor in crazy, circuitous patterns. Then we turned Kalli loose to track them. It should come as no surprise that she cleaned the floor in record time.

"So, nothing serious," I prompted her, watching her drop cookie bits around us. I lowered Kalli to the floor and returned my focus to the vet.

Terri shrugged. "You say she's been doing agility. I think she just strained her shoulder on some piece of the equipment. Probably jammed it. Try to keep her quiet for the next few days."

I shook my head. "Why do you vets always say that? You know, dog owners the world over think our vets are out of their minds when we hear those words. Like it's possible to keep an active dog quiet!"

Terri laughed. "I know it's crazy to expect. Just do your best. Try little things like lifting her out of the car rather than letting her jump down to the ground, for example. You have a walk-out from the lower level of your house, and that's where your office is, right? So, when you're going to work in the morning, take her around the outside rather than letting her scramble on the stairs. Stuff like that. Oh, and you might also try getting her adjusted."

"Adjusted?"

"Right. A colleague of mine—also a vet—specializes in chiropractic adjustment and acupuncture. I think Kay would be perfect for Kalli. Are you open to trying something like that?"

"Absolutely," I said without hesitation. I'd been concerned Terri was going to prescribe drugs for Kalli. My orientation when it came to my own health—and those of my loved ones—was to focus on holistic, non-invasive procedures. Given the hitch in Kalli's shoulder, an adjustment made perfect sense.

Clutching Kay's phone number, I escorted Kalli from the vet's office. She bounced next to me as if nothing in the world was wrong. I watched her even gait as she trotted toward the car. "Showing off for Terri, eh? Well, she's not looking at you. She's already seeing her next patient."

With her next step, Kalli began to favor her right front leg once again. Coincidence that this occurred immediately after my words to her? I think not.

Even though Terri's pronouncement was not in the least bit dire, I still worried about Kalli and winced with her every limping step. I called Kay immediately. It was Friday afternoon.

I heard nothing from her the rest of that day, nor on Saturday. Accustomed to vets who returned my phone calls promptly, I wasn't pleased with Kay's lack of response.

"I can't believe she hasn't called yet," I exploded to Marc on Sunday afternoon.

"Laura, it's a weekend. She probably won't even get her messages until Monday morning."

"But, what if there was an emergency? How would she handle that?"

"She's not a primary care vet. There's an assumption that you have a regular vet who referred you to her. Right?"

I hated it when he made so much sense. I looked over to see Kalli grinning at me. "All right," I snapped at her. "Alpha Dad makes a good point. What of it? Don't you have a rawhide bone to chew?"

Hmmph! Just because Daddy called you out on your nonsense, don't take it out on me. I tried to tell you my shoulder is no big deal. But would you listen to me? No! And now, you won't even listen to other humans.

As for this Kay person, I'm sensing she's good people, but she's really busy and being pulled in lots of different directions. Kinda like you were when we were packing for Colorado. She'll get back to you. Just not on your schedule. On hers.

Chill, Mom. Not everything is life and death.

By Monday morning, I still hadn't heard from Kay. If she hadn't been recommended to me by a person I trusted, I would have sought the services of someone else. But as it was, if Terri vouched for Kay, that was good enough for me.

Unfortunately, Terri could do nothing about my impatience. Against my better judgment, I called Kay on Monday afternoon and left a terse message. Okay, so it was more anger-filled than terse. But I was looking out for my little girl, I rationalized as my conscience shrieked at me for my bad behavior.

Marc just shook his head at me. "Laura, I know your world revolves around Kalli, but you can't expect Kay to feel the same way. She's juggling the demands of many owners with ailing pets…not just you and Kalli. I gotta tell you, if I were Kay, I'd never respond to you now. Not after that rant."

A twinge of guilt crept through my frustration. "I know. I know." I sighed, trying to stuff down my emotions. "Well, if I don't hear from her by midweek, I'll know it was because of me, not her."

Wonders did happen. Especially when Kalli was involved.

Kay called me Tuesday afternoon. I could tell from the tone of this perfect stranger's voice that she was doing her best to be polite. I guessed she was willing to proceed with an appointment because Terri had referred me. She agreed to see Kalli and me the next afternoon at the house.

I was still beating myself up for my unreasonable behavior when she rang the doorbell. I opened the door and exploded into an apology. She froze, stared at me as she listened to my every word, then burst into laughter.

When Kay had calmed a bit, she sputtered, "I have to be honest with you. I almost didn't call you after listening to your last message. But then I realized what I was hearing was more fear than anger. You obviously love your dog very much." She dropped to her knees before Kalli and said in a formal tone, "And how do you do, Miss Kalli?"

I liked this woman immediately. She understood what was important and was willing to overlook almost everything else. I took a moment to observe her. She was about my age, I estimated, with a thick French braid running down her back, a slender frame shorter than mine, and sparkling eyes. She had the air of a horsewoman. Later, I was to learn my instincts were right on the button. Kay was an accomplished rider, owned fifteen horses, and focused much of her practice on the equine population in the Denver foothills.

I could tell Kalli liked what she saw, too. She performed her "I trust you" maneuver by turning around so her wiggling butt faced the vet.

Kay giggled. "Oh, you're one of those, are you?" Without hesitation, she planted a hand by the base of Kalli's tail and scratched her in all the right spots. Kalli was in heaven.

Oh, man. I told you she was good folks, Mom. And she really knows how to handle me. She's great!

Now, try to behave yourself and not piss her off. She's given you a second chance. For both our sakes, don't screw it up.

I noticed after a few minutes, Kay was doing more than scratching. She had gradually moved her hands up to Kalli's shoulders and was more manipulating than petting my dog.

She broke off and looked up at me. "Let's put her on a leash and walk her around outside a bit. I'd like to see how she's moving."

Kalli and I complied under Kay's watchful eye. I heard a few thoughtful "hmm's" coming from the deck where she stood. Finally she called out, "Okay, I see what's going on. Let's take her back inside."

As soon as we entered the house, Kay dropped to the floor in the front hallway, her back against the door. With Kalli facing away from her, she pulled my dog between her legs and then bent her knees, effectively boxing in Kalli on both sides.

"Very effective." I nodded.

Kay smiled and her whole face lit up. "Yeah. You learn how to corral them after a while."

Kalli contributed to the conversation with a butt wiggle.

I noticed that as Kay talked, her hands roved across Kalli's body. Then they settled at her shoulder blades. With quick tweaks, they manipulated the bones, then worked their way down Kalli's back. It was fascinating to watch. Kay's hands seemed to have a mind of their own, and she was content to let them have their way.

After a few minutes, Kalli grew restless, shifting uneasily between Kay's legs. Kay immediately let her go and Kalli trotted off to the living room, where she took up position with her legs spread and had herself a good shake.

"Good job," caroled Kay. She turned to me with a smile. "She's doing great."

"So, was she out of alignment?"

"Yep. Definitely stuck just behind her right shoulder blade. Which is why she was favoring that leg. The limp should fade over time. I'll follow up with her in a few weeks, just to make sure all is well."

Kalli did, indeed, improve. And after a few more visits, Kay ascertained the adjustment was holding and Kalli was good as new.

Which is the way she continued to be for the next few years. Indeed, Marc and I almost forgot about Kalli's jammed shoulder until late one evening when Kalli, who had been lying at my feet chewing a rawhide stick, suddenly jerked to her feet with a whimper.

Marc and I looked at her in amazement as she streaked around the room, favoring her right front leg as she ran, her head cocked at an odd angle to the right. We tried to calm her, but she grew frantic and couldn't be stilled.

Tears in my eyes, I stared at Marc. "What on earth?"

He shook his head, clearly as distressed as I was. "We need to get her to the vet. She's clearly in terrible pain."

The thirty-minute trip to the emergency vet clinic seemed to take forever as I sat in the back seat with Kalli and tried to control her jerking movements. She appeared to be almost blinded by the pain, completely unaware of what she was doing. I was concerned her random thrashing would hurt her further.

The clinic receptionist took one look at her and ushered us into an examining room immediately. "The vet will be right in."

Marc and I watched Kalli with a sinking feeling. There is no greater hell than watching someone you love in terrible distress when there's nothing you can do to help.

"Do you think this is related to the shoulder jam she had a few years ago?" Marc asked in strained tones just as the veterinarian entered the room.

The doctor's eyes honed in on Kalli. "Tell me about the shoulder jam," he said in a controlled voice.

We briefed him as he knelt by Kalli and began to manipulate her neck and shoulders. When he reached the base of her neck, she screamed.

"It's a disc," he murmured, rising and releasing her. He turned toward me. "Hold her in place. I'm going to her something to make her more comfortable."

"Disc?" I looked at Marc.

"Makes sense. Look at the way she's holding her head. The source of pain is definitely in the lower neck area."

The vet returned and confirmed what Marc had just said. "We need to get a look at her spine to see what's going on. I'm recommending that you keep her here for the next few days so we can use a myelogram to study her."

"A what?" I asked. Even the word sounded painful.

The vet explained that a myelogram was a diagnostic procedure in which dye is injected into the spinal column in the dog's lower back. In normal dogs, the dye flows evenly along the spinal cord toward the head. If issues exist with a disc, the dye will not flow into the affected area, thus pinpointing the problem.

"She'll have to have general anesthesia," the vet informed us in a serious voice. "Is that an issue for you?"

Marc and I looked at each other. I could see my helpless feeling mirrored in his eyes. I nodded in response to his silent question, and Marc turned back to the vet. "Do what you need to do. She can't continue like this."

I couldn't remember a more heart-wrenching experience than leaving Kalli at that clinic, knowing she was suffering and had a major surgical procedure awaiting her.

"We're doing what needs to be done, Laura," Marc said in a quiet voice as we drove home. "We'll sort this out. You'll see."

I nodded, unable to speak.

I'd managed to keep tears at bay. But when I walked into the house and saw Kalli's toys strewn on the family room carpet around her well-worn and much-loved bed, I lost it and started sobbing. Marc wrapped his arms around me and let me cry it out. And while I felt much better after the last tear had been shed, my worry didn't ease at all.

Our mood improved a few days later when the vet called us. "She's doing great," he said in a cheerful voice. "It appears one of the discs has calcified from an injury she sustained in the past. Probably in the last year or two. Perhaps related to that jammed shoulder you told me about. Anyway, that damaged disc swelled recently."

"What would cause the swelling?" I asked.

"Hard to say. She could have turned her head and caught it just so. But the point is, the swelling pressed on a nerve in her neck, which is what caused the pain. The good news is it wasn't pressing on her spine. And now that the swelling has gone down, she's back to normal. Let's schedule an appointment for tomorrow. You can pick her up, and I'll show you the test results. We can talk more then."

I took a deep breath as I put down the phone. It was the first time I'd been able to inhale without heartache in the last few days.

The next afternoon, Marc and I entered the veterinarian examining room to find Kalli wiggling toward us as if the horrific days of pain had never occurred.

"So, how do we keep this from happening again?" Marc asked the doctor.

"The best thing you can do is keep her adjusted. If her spine stays in alignment, odds are good the inflammation that caused the pain won't occur. Do you have a chiropractor?"

I nodded, thinking about Kay.

"Good. Beyond that, I suggest you keep her from putting pressure on her shoulders, which is what happens when she jumps off the bed or couch, or from your car. You might even restrict how much she goes down stairs. I'd also place her food and water bowls on a raised stand, so she doesn't have to lower her head when she eats and drinks. Oh, and use a harness when you have her on leash. You don't want to pull on her neck if you can help it."

Marc and I nodded, obedient and determined to do whatever we could to keep Kalli healthy and comfortable. We purchased a harness, food bowl stand, and called Kay.

Then, the three of us collapsed. Kalli was still worn out from her clinic visit. Marc and I were emotionally exhausted.

Okay, I gotta tell you, Mommy...that was totally unacceptable. It was like the pain come out of nowhere. And to be honest, I'm terrified it's going to happen again. I'm really scared, Mommy.

Look, I know you're not responsible for what caused it, but can you at least protect me from it in the future? Because I don't want to feel that way again. And I don't want to go back to that place, either. They were nice enough, but they gave me something that made me all woozy and out of control. Now, you know I hate feeling out of control. It just made everything so much ickier. Although, I gotta say I made them feel reeeeeaaaally sorry for me so they gave me extra treats.

At least I got something out of it. Siiiiiigh.

Why don't you call Kay and see if she can help? She does something with my bones that always makes me feel better.

ON SHAKY GROUND

And thus began a regimen that saw us welcoming Kay into our home twice every month for the rest of Kalli's life. The first appointment after Kalli's procedure proved to be a long one as Kay reviewed the vet's report in detail and we discussed my little dog's condition.

Sprawled on the floor in the entranceway, her back against the front door, Kay looked up from the paperwork, one arm outstretched as she scratched Kalli's butt. "I can understand why this guy wanted Kalli to be adjusted regularly." She waved the paperwork through the air. "That could make all the difference."

Kalli backed into Kay so the scratching could migrate to a different spot.

Kay laughed. "Well, it seems Kalli knows what to do." But as Kay put down the paper and started to manipulate Kalli, I could see my dog freeze. Her carefree manner was gone. Fear had replaced it.

"Kay…"

"I know. She's worried about what I'm going to do. Remember, she's really been through the wringer over the last few weeks. That pain is fresh in her mind, and even though she doesn't feel it at the moment, she's scared it will return."

"How do you know all that?"

Kay paused, as if searching for words, then said simply, "Because I sense it."

"Oh?"

Kay laughed. "Don't look at me like I've grown a second head. You sensed it, too."

"I don't know that I *sensed* it. More like, I just know my dog." I shrugged.

Kay gave me a long look. "And that knowing? Where do you suppose that comes from?"

"From living with her for years."

"Really? That's all your 'knowing' is? Familiarity?"

I started to affirm that, then paused. Suddenly, I wasn't sure.

Kay went on. "Because I perceive your little dog is an awesome communicator. She's very clear. Even to people who haven't known her for years."

"Huh?" I squeaked. This conversation was taking an odd turn that made me very uncomfortable.

"Yup," Kay went on. "And it works the other way, too. She knows exactly what I'm doing and why. I suppose some people would call that uncanny."

"But not you?"

"There's nothing uncanny about it. It's perfectly natural. Animals communicate with us all the time. They speak to us and understand when we speak to them. It's just that most people don't pay attention, or are unwilling to pick up on the process."

My mind flashed to a television program I'd watched a few days before on the Animal Planet Channel: *Pet Psychic*. The program profiled a woman who claimed to be able to communicate with animals…actually hearing their thoughts and responding to them in kind. The cynic in me wanted to laugh at the notion one could talk directly to an animal, but there was a part of me that wondered if the woman was legit. Especially after what Kay had just said.

And if I were completely honest with myself, I'd have to admit that after years of watching Kalli interact with humans and canines, alike, I'd always believed she seemed aware of far more than most people credited dogs with knowing. However, I wasn't sure if I felt comfortable believing she could actually read minds, or that she could talk to mine.

In a studied, casual tone, I mentioned watching the *Pet Psychic*. Then I waited for Kay's reaction.

"Oh, yeah. I watch that show all the time. That lady is definitely for real."

I looked at Kay closely. I'd known her long enough to realize she didn't make a comment like that lightly.

Ha! Now you really started something, Mom. But it's good you did because this opening-yourself-up thing is very important.

All this time, I've been talking to you. And while your instincts accepted it within the first week I moved in with you and Daddy—thanks to my brilliance at communicating, of course—the rest of you didn't have a clue you were hearing me. You've gotten a bit better recently, but even at your best, only a teensy part of you picks up what I'm saying. Mostly, you don't have a clue.

I almost feel sorry for you...looking all confused right now.

You know, you should be better at this than you are. I mean, you of all people. Okay, so let's start with something familiar. Remember Carly's Group? How we dogs worked with their clients? How do you suppose we knew just what to do and when to do it? Guesswork? Dumb luck? Coincidence?

Puleeeeaase.

Really, we dogs are far more advanced than you humans. You guys have so much standing in the way of your paying attention. Your ears hear only so much and then you turn off the sound. And the same with the rest of your senses. Too much input and you turn tail and run from your instincts.

We animals? We're tuned in all the time. We accept the energy that's sent out by every living thing every minute of every day. We learn to work with it, sharing it with those of you who choose to be open to its existence.

And that means we can heal and teach and... Well, there's no limit, really.

Hmmmmm? Too much information? Sorry. Kay and I will take this in baby steps for you.

I continued staring at Kay, and she laughed easily. "Just think about what we've discussed. And consider the lady on *Pet Psychic*. Let the idea of animal communication settle. Don't try to force it." She winked at me. "I'm betting your intuition will tell you all you need to know."

I did exactly what Kay suggested. Over the course of the next few weeks, I thought about our conversation long and hard. During that time, Kalli had an air of mild disgust about her. I tried telling myself I was imagining that.

And then the notion of animal communication ratcheted to a new level for Marc and me. All because of Bailey.

Bailey was a Weimaraner who had lived across the street from us in Evanston. She and Kalli had been the best of friends. Well, she'd been friends with Kalli. In turn, Kalli had tolerated her. Which was more than Kalli would do with most dogs. So when I received a call about Bailey from Maris, an Evanston dog walker who had exercised both Kalli and Bailey from time to time, I listened carefully.

Bailey's humans had just had a baby. Bailey, less than thrilled with this disruption in her household, had begun to act out. Doggie poop and piddle had appeared throughout the house, along with chewed shoes. It was when Bailey started snapping at the baby that the couple appealed to Maris for help. They were at the end of their rope with two A.M. feedings and spells of colic. Could Maris find a loving home for Bailey?

Marc and I topped Maris's list of potential new parents for the Weimaraner. Were we interested in adopting the gray lady?

I had no idea how I felt about the prospect. Up to that point, I'd been convinced Kalli was a confirmed only dog in our household. But, this was *Bailey* we were talking about. Kalli knew her and got along with her. Was it possible we could expand our family with an additional dog?

Still holding the phone in one hand after my conversation with Maris had ended, I looked down at Kalli. Suddenly, I realized the most important opinion regarding Bailey belonged to the family member with four legs, not two. Because if my little dog wasn't on board with the idea, we'd have a disaster on our hands.

"Okay, kid. Kay tells me you understand what I'm saying. So, what do you think about this Bailey situation?"

Oh, man. I'd be happy to tell you, but I don't think you're ready to hear me yet. As usual, Mom, you're being the overachiever, jumping way out ahead of yourself instead of taking the learning curve in small, easy bits.

Hmmmm. How to explain this so you can begin to understand...

I've got it! Now I have to see if you can hear just this little bit. Maybe if I'm really, really loud...

REMEMBER YOUR FRIEND DINA? SHE CALLED AN ANIMAL COMMUNICATOR WHEN SHE HAD QUESTIONS ABOUT ONE OF HER DOGS. THAT COMMUNICATOR IS WHERE YOU WANT TO START.

Darn. I don't think I'm getting through to you. Looks like I need to simplify.

CALL DINA... CALL DINA... CALL DINA...

I stared at Kalli for a long moment. She stared back at me.

Suddenly, the image of Dina popped into my mind. And the memory of a recent telephone conversation I'd had with her. She had told me one of her dogs—a deaf rescue Aussie named Nicky—had developed some alarming behavioral issues over the last few months. Being a trainer, Dina had been confident she could address the problems on her own. But Nicky had been resistant to traditional techniques.

Dina had been at a loss. In desperation, she had contacted a local woman who claimed she was an animal communicator. Through Jenna, Dina had learned Nicky had been freaked during a recent thunderstorm. Not being able to hear the thunder, the Aussie was thrown off guard when he felt the vibrations from a nearby lightning strike. It had reminded him of an episode from his puppyhood in which he'd been terrified by lightning. This memory had thrown him into a tailspin, resulting in the behavioral problems.

Armed with this knowledge, Dina had been able to work with Nicky in an effective and loving way. Soon, he was back to normal.

I thought about how Dina—always pragmatic and logical—had accepted Jenna's information as fact and had proceeded to act based on that information. And how successful the outcome appeared to have been. Perhaps I could avail myself of Jenna's services, too.

I called Dina. As I was talking to her, I glanced down at Kalli. I could have sworn I saw a smug little smile on her face.

Nah. Just my imagination.

"Hey, I think that's a great idea," Dina said after I'd explained the situation to her. "Jenna is super, Laura. If anyone can get inside the head of that crafty dog of yours, it'll be her."

"So, you really believe Jenna was able to talk to Nicky?"

"You've seen how Nicky has changed since I learned about the lightning strike. There's no way I would have figured that out without Jenna's help."

"But perhaps it was just a lucky guess on Jenna's part. I mean, a lot of dogs are afraid of thunderstorms. How much of a reach would it have been for her to throw that out?" I winced as soon as the words came out of my mouth.

Kalli harrumphed and left the room.

"Funny. I thought you'd be more open to the idea of animal communication," Dina said.

I sighed. "I am, really. It's just the cynical part of me that's rebelling against it."

"What do your instincts tell you?"

Now Dina was sounding like Kay. What was this, a conspiracy? I hesitated, searching for words, wanting to tell Dina the absolute truth, even if I wasn't entirely sure what that was. "My instincts tell me it's possible."

Dina hooted with laughter. "You really are playing the skeptic, aren't you? Okay, I'll stop picking on you. But I do have a suggestion."

"What?"

"Call Jenna. Give her a try. See what she has to say, then judge for yourself."

Right. That made perfect sense. I promised Dina I'd do just that and hung up.

For long moments, I stared at the paper on which I'd scrawled Jenna's phone number. Dina had told me the woman didn't have to be in the room with Kalli in order to "talk" to her, that she could reach out to Kalli over the phone because what she was doing was "energy" work. Whatever *that* meant. All I had to do was schedule a day and time for a phone conference.

All I had to do…

Yep. Not much to do at all.

Really.

Suddenly, a nagging sensation swept over me. It felt like pressure coming from the inside, pushing me into action. I'd had the sensation before to a lesser degree. Like when it was time for Kalli's walk or her dinner, or it was a hot day in the park and I just knew Kalli and I needed to make a beeline for the air-conditioned car.

Now that I thought about it, I felt that pressure quite often. And it always involved Kalli.

Almost without realizing it, I found myself punching Jenna's number into the phone. How odd. I'd planned to wait a few days before I made the call. But there I was, standing in the kitchen, phone to ear, listening to it ring at the other end.

On the third ring, a pleasant female voice came on the line. I introduced myself to Jenna, being sure to mention Dina's name as the one who had referred the communicator to me.

"Oh, yes. Dina and Nicky. How is he doing? Was Dina able to sort out the thunderstorm thing?"

"Uh, yes. As a matter of fact, she's been able to work with him and now he's much better."

Listen to your own words, Mom. Did you hear yourself? Because of Jenna's insights as she listened to Nicky talk to her, Dina was able to help the dog.

Give it up, Mom. Time to surrender the doubts.

I looked down to see Kalli had reentered the room and was sprawling across my feet.

"So, how can I help you?" came Jenna's voice.

"Well, um." I hesitated. And the longer I paused, the more pressure built up inside me. The only thing I could do to relieve it was to talk to this woman.

And so I did.

Almost as if I was listening to someone else speak, in a voice that seemed a million miles away, I blurted out the situation with Bailey and Kalli. I paused to catch my breath, then added, "So, if you have some time available, I'd like to consult with you." I added hastily, "And Kalli, of course."

Bravo, Mom! Bravo.

Jenna chuckled. "I can hear your dog is pleased you called me."

"Excuse me?"

"Oh, yes, she's been cheering you in the background." Jenna paused. "But then, I think on some level you knew that. As for consulting about the dogs, no time like the present. What would you like me to ask Kalli?"

I froze. I hadn't expected to talk to her on the spot. A wave of nervousness swept over me. Vaguely, I heard Jenna start to laugh.

"Oh, your dog is really something," she sputtered. "You want to know what she just told me?"

"Sure." *Did I?*

"She told me I could save my questions. That she would tell me everything I needed to know." Jenna chortled. "Does that sound like your dog?"

I laughed in spite of my nervousness. "Oh, yeah. That's pure Kalli."

"She does have a message for someone else in your household. Alpha Dad?"

A thrill of excitement shot through me. No one but Kalli could have told Jenna about that nickname for Marc. My...God. Maybe Kalli really *was* talking to this woman. My voice sounded tight as I heard myself say, "Yes, she's referring to my husband, Marc."

"And he has the habit of saying to her, 'Oh, Kalli. You're *just* a dog.' Right?"

My head was swimming. I couldn't believe what I was hearing. Indeed, Marc said that to her all the time. I heard myself stutter, "R...r...right."

Jenna went on, "Well, Kalli wants him to know that while she doesn't mind if he refers to her as a dog, she really does object to him characterizing her as *just* a dog. In fact, she'd like to remind him she's really far *more* than a dog."

I'll say, more than a dog. "Wow, Jenna. This is amazing."

"Not really, dear. I'm simply listening to Kalli and relaying what she's telling me. She's very articulate and sophisticated in the way she talks to me, by the way. You know, a communicator can only pick up what a dog, or horse, or cat, or whatever, is capable of 'saying.' Some animals are able to convey only rough, primitive word pictures. And some can only grunt. Others, like your Kalli, can actually talk in complete sentences I hear in my head."

"Okay." I was trying to keep up with Kalli and Jenna. Really, I was. But honestly, I was overwhelmed. I knew I'd have a lot to process once the conversation ended. I took a deep breath. "So, what about Bailey? What does Kalli think about her moving in with us?"

Silence descended on the phone line, broken by the occasional chuckle and "hmmm" from Jenna. Finally, she said, "Well, Kalli doesn't particularly like Bailey. Actually, to be more accurate, I should say she doesn't respect Bailey. In fact, she considers the dog to be quite beneath her— Hmmm? What, Kalli?" More silence. "Right, I'll tell her."

"Tell me what?"

"Kalli feels sorry for Bailey. And she realizes Bailey needs a new home. Things have been bad with Bailey's humans for some time now. And while Kalli isn't crazy to have her around all the time, if she can help out the dog, she's willing to."

Mom, I know, you're thinking about how Bailey and I used to lie side by side on our front lawn and appeared perfectly happy together. You thought that was really cute. And you just assumed we were best buddies. I guess I can understand how you'd make that mistake.

Nothing could be further from the truth. Geesh, Mom. I don't know how I can be any clearer. The truth is, I think Bailey is one of the most pathetic dogs I've ever met. That's why I tolerated her the way I did. And that's why I'd accept her into our home if she has no other place to go. It's the least I can do for such a sad sack of an animal in a bad situation.

Now, I've explained this to Jenna, and she gets it. Sorta. But I'm afraid she's struggling a bit. I have to talk reeeeeeeaaaaally slow to her, or she just doesn't understand all I'm trying to tell her. It sure would be easier if you could get your act together and hear me yourself. I'm betting you'd be much better at it than she is. If you just opened yourself to me...

As the minutes ticked by, I became increasingly comfortable with the three-way conversation. Questions buzzed in my head. With great patience, Jenna answered each on behalf of my little dog. Nothing remarkable was revealed until I asked Kalli, through Jenna, how she had felt about her therapy work with the "Urban Sisters" project. I hadn't actively pursued animal-assisted therapy with Kalli since we'd moved to Colorado, and I was contemplating joining a program at a major medical center in Denver.

"She hated it."

I froze, staring at the phone receiver and then Kalli, who seemed to be dozing on the floor next to me.

"Carly's Group? She hated Carly's Group?"

"Oh, yeah. Something about teenage girls who really annoyed her."

Kalli opened her eyes to look at me, and I could have sworn she winked before she settled back into her nap.

"But she was so good at— What else does she have to say about it?" My voice was weak, my thoughts spinning.

"Kalli participated in the program to please you. She knew it was important to you. And she was willing to work with the girls because she realized they needed her and that she could do some good. But, given a choice, she'd have been far happier curling up next to you on the living room couch on those nights."

Suddenly, the image of Kalli sitting by the revolving doors of the girls' residence facility, waiting for me to take her home, flooded my mind's eye. I tuned into that image and it became animated, as if I were watching a home movie in my head. I saw Kalli's look of disgust as I walked her back into the conference room that night. I saw how she'd been cooperative and biddable as she obeyed me and the girls throughout each therapy session, but how, as soon as she'd been released from a command, she'd always raced for the door and looked back at me expectantly.

I'd even acknowledged that she was less than pleased with Carly's Group at the time. But I'd stuffed my inner voice in favor of pursuing a path I felt was worthwhile…for both of us.

Oh, geesh, Mom. Don't get all twisted out of shape over this Carly's Group thing. It's not that big a deal, and it wasn't at the time. I wouldn't have said anything about it at all if this lady person hadn't asked me a specific question.

Of course, if you'd pushed the therapy thing here in Colorado, I would have had to tell you how I feel about it. I'm getting older, you know. I'm just not willing to extend myself for that kind of stuff any longer. Takes too much out of me.

Listen, don't make me into a monster just because I didn't love therapy work as much as you did. I was bored by it. And you know how I hate being bored. But, I got the point of it, so I did my best. And, hey, I was pretty darned good, if I do say so myself.

Let it go. Don't beat yourself up, and please don't judge me.

Suddenly, a feeling of peace swept over me. Kalli's reaction to Carly's Group work had been fair. And the satisfaction I'd derived from it had been fair, as well.

I stroked Kalli's head. "Thank you, sweetheart, for doing such a magnificent job for those girls. You might not have been thrilled about what you were doing, but you made a real difference. And that's a gift from you that I honor."

Kalli fixed me with a concentrated stare. Maybe I was getting caught up with the weird animal communication thing going on with Jenna, but suddenly, I knew exactly what Kalli was thinking behind her focused eyes.

"No, love. We aren't going to participate in the Children's Hospital therapy program. I get it. You're done."

She heaved a huge sigh—of relief?

It was time to end the session. I hung up the phone, noticing Kalli had moved across the room to nestle in her bed by the fireplace. Now, she was looking pleased with herself. "Well, my dear. This has been quite the afternoon. I knew you were brilliant, of course. But really, Kalli. *Talking* to Jenna? *Really?*"

Really, Mom. Really.

Head spinning, I sank onto the couch, studying my dog. I'd begun the conversation with Jenna feeling skeptical. In a matter of minutes, I had become...hmm...what was I now? A less-entrenched skeptic? A believer? I wasn't sure. But I was open-minded enough to acknowledge the truthfulness of what had just transpired between Jenna and Kalli...and me.

And I knew a huge shift had occurred in my thinking.

After Marc came home from the office later that day, I told him about Jenna. He shook his head at me. "You don't really believe this nonsense, do you?"

"You have to admit, what Jenna said was compelling."

"And now you're going to say she couldn't have made up the bit about my 'just a dog' comment. Right?"

"Well, yeah. I mean, how could she have guessed that…" I trailed off and glanced at Kalli. She was fixing Marc with that same intense stare she'd given me earlier in the day. "I gotta say, there's something about all of this that makes some sense. See how Kalli's focused on you? It's like she knows what you're saying, that you're doubtful."

Marc looked over at her and then back at me, then shrugged. "Okay, so I have to admit, there have been times when I've felt she knew what we were saying. And I mean, beyond the standard verbal commands."

"Ah, ha!" I felt like I'd scored a huge victory.

"But still…"

"Hey, Marc? Why don't you play it safe and knock it off with the '*just* a dog' thing."

He nodded slowly. "Right."

We also honored Kalli by electing not to adopt Bailey. In the end, that decision turned out to be a good one for all concerned as Maris found a marvelous home for the Weimaraner in Evanston.

The concept of animal communication was reinforced in an unexpected way through a friend I'd made in a Denver writers group. There was nothing about Anita that alerted me to her psychic life when I first met her. She was an older woman with gleaming white hair and a penchant for writing gritty murder mysteries. After attending several critique sessions, I noticed that the group had no idea what to do with her. The concept of a silver-haired grandma turning out scenes filled with blood and gore just didn't compute for them. I, on the other hand, found her intriguing. And so did Kalli.

I could tell my little dog liked her the minute she walked into the house one sunny January afternoon. I'd invited Anita for brunch, and the quiche was bubbling in the oven as I introduced her to Kalli.

Rather than ooh and aah over the spaniel, which is what just about everyone did upon first laying eyes on my exceptionally cute dog, Anita ignored her.

Not being accustomed to this behavior, Kalli pressed her nose against Anita's leg once my friend had settled in an armchair by the family room fireplace. Anita continued chatting easily, acting as if Kalli didn't exist. With a "humph," Kalli dropped to the floor at Anita's feet and started at her steadily.

I half-listened to Anita's words, too busy wondering if she was ever going to pet my dog to really pay attention to the conversation.

Well, gee. You're not the only one wondering if she's ever going to pet me. I can't believe she'd ignore such a gorgeous, brilliant animal such as m—

Hmmm? Wait. Who's talking to me? Is that you, Mommy's guest?

Wow. You're really hearing me and— What?

Oooohhh. I see. You're one of those humans who's really tuned in to us creatures. Well, they're creatures. I'm a Kalli.

Yeah, you may think that's funny, but after you're around me for a while, you'll see what I mean.

Right, I speak in sentences. None of those crude word pictures for me. I'm the real deal.

You know, I just realized you're asking me about Mommy while you're talking to her! Wow. You're really good. I'm not easily impressed by humans, but you're different.

Yes, to answer your question. She's kinda figuring out this communication thing in her own, limited way. She's not even close to picking me up like you do. For example, she has no idea we're talking like this because on the surface, you're focused on her and seem to be ignoring me.

Hmmm? Right. I think that's a good idea. Working with Mommy slowly over time is the best way to go with her. She's a real overachiever.

Say, there's something I'd like to know. Why haven't you petted me yet? You appear to be ignoring me.

...establishing your alpha status? Oh, I see. You had me figured out before you even laid eyes on me. And you're right. I would have tested you if you'd given me half a chance. I am, after all, a very bright more-than-a-dog.

In mid-sentence, Anita reached down and laid a hand on Kalli's head. My dog, in turn, looked up at her with complete adoration.

We continued to chat about the writers group, but it was Anita's unusual attitude toward my dog that had really piqued my interest. Finally, I spoke up and asked her why she'd ignored Kalli when she first entered the house.

Anita smiled. "Yes, I knew you were wondering about that."

I froze. Oh, Lord. People weren't just "talking" to animals, any longer. Now, they were reading my mind.

"It's not really reading your mind," Anita replied to words I hadn't verbalized. "You're broadcasting your thoughts. In fact, you're actually quite loud. You must have known I have certain…hmm… I guess you could call them gifts." She chuckled. "Although there are days when I question the use of that word." She learned toward me. "I'm an intuitive, honey. Come from a long line of psychics going back generations. I'm one of those folks who communicate with Guides. And keep in mind, we all have Guides. It's just that some of us are more tuned in to them than others. So, I 'hear' things from my Council, and I can see energy patterns that radiate around people, and—"

"You mean their auras?" My mind was reeling.

"That's exactly right. *And* I can pick up messages from animals."

I sank back in my chair after first making certain my feet were still planted firmly on the carpeting. My world was turning upside down from the way I'd always looked at it.

I stared at my dog. It was all Kalli's fault.

"Oh, I know you're shocked. At least on one level. But you're much more open to this than you think," Anita continued, watching me with bright blue eyes. "And you're more aware than you know."

I glanced back at Kalli, and I could have sworn she winked at me. "Ever since my vet-friend, Kay, and I talked about the *Pet Psychic* TV program, I feel as if I'm living in an episode of a different show— *Twilight Zone.*"

"Just take it easy," Anita replied. "Don't force it." She glanced over at Kalli and fell silent for a long moment, then she turned back to me. "Your dog is concerned about you. Afraid you'll miss out on 'important stuff,' as she put it, if you don't open your mind. Apparently, she thinks you're ready to accept a whole new dimension to life. And frankly, I'm not going to argue with her."

"Yeah, she can be intimidating at times."

"You really are very psychic, Laura. But you were taught to shut down the instinct when you were little. Your family found your gifts frightening, so they sabotaged you. Does that make sense?"

In spite of my trepidation as I stepped into uncharted territory, Anita's words had resonated with me. "Yes, it does make sense," I heard myself say.

Kalli rose from her position at Anita's feet and walked over to me. Very carefully, she sat next to my legs and pressed against me.

"She's processing for you." Anita nodded toward her.

"Okay, enough mystery. Tell me what you're talking about." I winced because my voice sounded a bit strident

"Animals process for their humans all the time, Laura," Anita said in quiet tones. "What do I mean by that? Well, let's start at the beginning. You know our pets are gifts from God."

"Absolutely." All one had to do was look into Kalli's face to believe that.

"And they volunteer to come to us in our lifetimes."

I nodded. I recognized the veracity of what she was saying.

She went on. "When they volunteer, they agree to work with us and teach us. And indeed, we learn from them in all sorts of way, especially as we watch them interact with the world around them. For example, during a walk, they show us how to appreciate nature. To notice all the little things we'd miss otherwise in our busy lives."

Suddenly, the image came to mind of Marc and me taking Kalli out to our backyard in Evanston as we potty trained her. I remembered how Kalli had paused to sniff each blade of grass. At the time, I'd suspected that much of her behavior had been a hustle, designed to manipulate us so she could avoid going back into her kitchen kennel. But as I reflected on Anita's words, I realized those outside stints spoke to more than Kalli's brilliant calculation. They also represented a lesson that had urged Marc and me to slow down and savor the tiny details of our yard.

Anita was nodding. "Yes, you and Marc have received wonderful lessons from Kalli. But she's here to do more than teach. Kalli's also very serious about helping you. She senses you're upset and confused, so she's absorbing the negative energy you're generating, removing it from you."

"That's why she's pressing up against me like this?"

"Well, that physical contact is helping both of you, it's true. But she doesn't have to touch you in order to process for you. It's energy work, Laura. Physical proximity isn't required to function on an energetic level."

I remembered Jenna trying to explain to me how she could communicate with Kalli from a distance. Looking at Anita, I remained silent, figuring she'd just picked up on my thoughts.

Sure enough, she nodded and smiled at me. "Very good," she said in a quiet voice. "You're beginning to get the hang of this."

Kalli sighed and flopped onto my feet. Eyes closed, she fell fast asleep. Her gentle snores and steady breathing filled the room. Suddenly, I felt content and peaceful.

Feeling a bit silly, I nevertheless decided to describe this sensation to Anita. "Yes, you're picking up her mood," my friend replied. "She's very happy right now. She really does love to see you succeed, you know. And you've had a breakthrough, after all. She's glad for it."

"Breakthrough?" I thought about all that had transpired since Anita had first set foot in the house just minutes earlier. "I guess I have, haven't I?"

"And your little dog is exhausted. She just did a lot of work on your behalf."

After that afternoon with Anita, I never looked at Kalli the same way. Anita's comments had crystallized the disparate bits and pieces I'd picked up from Kay, Jenna, and the *Pet Psychic*. Suddenly, recognizing Kalli was tuned in to me and Marc, capable of reading us and speaking to us, didn't seem odd. It seemed…natural.

And so it was that from that point on, conversations I had with Anita—whether on the phone or in person—were punctuated by thoughts coming from a third party: Kalli. It wasn't at all unusual for Anita and I to be in the midst of talking about…whatever…when all of a sudden, Anita would pause. I knew that in those moments, Kalli was chiming in, adding her two cents to the topic at hand. Other times, Kalli would appear to be sound asleep in her bed, then suddenly lift her head and utter a series of *woofs*—her contribution to our conversation. Not quite facile enough to interpret her sounds, I'd wait for Anita to translate.

That was when I learned what an opinionated smartie she was, and what a salty vocabulary she had. Fleetingly, I wondered where she'd picked up some of those words. Then I realized she'd been listening to Marc and me for years.

It also became obvious that even an animal communicator could still be hustled by my dog. Anita proved that during one of her stints Kalli-sitting when Marc and I left town on family business.

As soon as we walked through the front door upon our return home, Anita launched into a rundown of all the Kalli events we'd missed while we were away. I could tell she'd saved the best story for last when she leaned forward in her chair with a bright gleam in her eyes and said, "You're not going to believe what your little girl did a few days ago."

Marc and I looked at each other without saying a word. We knew better than to even try to guess what Anita was going to say. And we'd lived with Kalli long enough to know it was going to be entertaining. We settled back and waited for Anita to begin her story.

She told us that early one evening, she settled on the couch with her favorite snack, arranging bowls of salsa and sour cream on the coffee table in front of her, and placing a bag of blue corn chips on the floor next to her feet. As soon as the bag hit the carpet, Kalli's head poked up and she rose from the spot in her bed where she'd been curled, seemingly asleep.

Anita watched her approach, but didn't move the chips from the floor, curious to see what Kalli would do about the food. Kalli eyed the bag, then laid down next to it. She didn't make a move toward it. Anita picked up the bag, took a handful of chips and then deposited it on the floor in its original position. Kalli yawned and glanced at Anita. Again, she made no move toward it.

Anita sat back and leisurely munched on her snack while watching the television with one eye and Kalli with the other. My dog yawned again and rolled over onto her side. Then Anita rose from the couch and stepped across the room to turn on a lamp.

Even with Anita physically separated from the bag, Kalli still showed no interest in stealing the food.

Now, Anita is one of the savvier people in the world when it comes to dealing with animals. And her ability to "read" them makes her an especially daunting human for a dog to try to hustle. But Kalli was up to the challenge.

For her part, Anita was convinced she had given Kalli plenty of opportunity to avail herself of the chips, and the dog hadn't taken the bait. Anita figured, therefore, that all would be well if she were to walk out of the room for a minute or two. Which is exactly what she did.

By the time Anita had reached the other end of the hallway, paper began rustling as Kalli dove for the chips. Anita reentered the room to find a spaniel head buried in the bag that was now lying on its side. Kalli barely acknowledged Anita was back in the room as she munched on the blue corn goodies, completely unconcerned she'd violated

Anita's trust in her.

In true Anita fashion, she found the incident hilarious and wiped tears from her eyes. "I'm telling you, she really got me good," Anita gasped. "And she was so smooth about it. She reasoned out the situation, observed what needed to be done to get what she wanted, and executed her plan with perfection. She was completely in control. And not a hint of remorse. I'm sure she figured I'd been the stupid one, so I got what I deserved." Our friend dissolved into another round of giggles. "It was a complete and glorious hustle. How many dogs could have pulled that off?" She shook her head. "I'm telling you, she's amazing."

Oh, please, it was nothing. For the life of me, I can't figure out why Anita thinks the whole incident was even worth mentioning. I mean, what about it is surprising? Did she really think I'd ignore the food? It wasn't a matter of whether I'd go after the chips, it was just a question of when I'd get them. They were really good, by the way.

And, hey, it's not like I haven't done that before. Remember the day in class when Kristen was silly enough to leave a tub of liver treats on the floor? I mean, she actually expected me to walk by it without touching anything. Talk about silly! And I showed her, didn't I?

MMMMmmm. They were yummy. Just about as good as Anita's chips.

You know, it's kinda weird, but Anita was almost easier to hustle than most other people because she couldn't imagine an animal pulling off anything like that with her. She completely underestimated me. And so I was really motivated. I'd never let a challenge like that go by without taking it on. And I have to say, getting the better of her was almost as much fun as eating the chips! The only thing I hated was the stupid bag making so much noise. Anita knew I was into it before I had a chance to eat very much.

Siiiiiigh. Oh well, I had fun, at least.

Kalli yawned and curled up on her bed. Clearly, the story was old news and bored my little dog.

SHIFTS IN PERCEPTION

One frigid wintry morning, I rose from my bed promptly at six o'clock, threw on clothes, and flung open Kalli's kennel door. Kalli bounded from the crate and gave herself a good shake. A few minutes later, we stood by the front door. I threw her red-checked flannel coat over her back and shrugged into my own parka. This was our usual start-of-a-winter's-day routine, comforting in its sameness.

As I let Kalli outside, I saw a fox trotting across the far end of the yard. Kalli hadn't noticed it, and I wanted to keep it that way, so I called to my dog in order to draw her away from the visitor.

Kalli continued moving forward, completely ignoring my command. I called to her again with the same result.

Suddenly, gales of yipping creased the frosty air as the little dogs living across the street tore out of a doggie door and raced onto their front deck.

Now, Kalli detested her canine neighbors. She and they had waged a war of "words" against each other ever since we'd moved into the house. And from that first moment, Kalli *never* missed an opportunity to hurl insults at them in response to their frenzied barking. It was obviously a matter of principle with her.

But, on this morning, Kalli completely ignored them as she nosed about our yard.

I froze in place, watching her sniff around the giant Ponderosa pine trees surrounding our house, looking for an appropriate place for her first piddle of the day. She didn't flinch; she didn't look up. It was as if the neighbor dogs weren't making a sound.

As if...

"Kalli?" She had her back to me and didn't turn around. I waited for her to squat and do her morning business. Then, when she shifted and was facing me, I raised an arm and gave her the hand signal for a recall. She promptly broke into a trot with a big smile and executed a perfect front and finish.

My heart had grown cold. Because the only explanation I could find for her not responding to my voice that morning was she couldn't hear it.

Overnight, Kalli had become deaf.

She bounced by my side as if nothing unusual was going on, wiggled her butt across the front door threshold, and waited for her breakfast in the kitchen. Everything she did was completely normal. She didn't appear distressed in the slightest, although she threw me a few concerned glances. I guessed she was picking up my panic.

Before she had finished the last morsel of her meal, I was on the phone with Anita. Kalli couldn't "tell" me what was going on, but my psychic friend could.

Anita grew quiet when I asked her the big question. Then the answer came. "I'm sorry, Laura, but you're absolutely right. She's deaf."

"But...but she was fine last night when we put her to bed." I told Anita about her annoyance with the yippy dogs across the street, how she made sure she always got in the last word. The battle occurring the night before had been typical of the ongoing verbal war between Kalli and those dogs.

"I know, honey," Anita said in a gentle voice. "She could hear them last night."

"How can she lose her hearing in one night?" I winced at my screeching tone and forced myself to take a deep breath.

"It happens."

"I'm sorry, but what kind of answer is that?"

"Laura, you can go to your vet, but she won't be able to tell you anything more than I have. Kalli did this for a reason."

"Okay, now you're not making any sense at all."

Anita sighed. "I'm not sure how much detail to give you." She paused, and I knew she was listening to her Guides. "Okay...remember when I told you that animals are brought to us from God to help us, to teach us?"

"Yeeees..."

"Well, it turns out you were assigned a Master Teacher. Kalli's one of the best. And for some reason, it was determined her going deaf would become an important point of growth for you. So, she agreed to it. Willingly."

"You're still not making sense to me."

Another pause on the other end of the phone. "Honey, I'm just relaying to you what I'm hearing."

"From your Guides, or her?"

"Both. She's not upset about it, by the way. In fact, she's getting a bit of a kick out of it." Anita chuckled. "Then again, she does love to shake you up. I'd say this qualifies."

Yeah, well she's still not getting it, Anita. How do we tell her I'm working with her Guides? That this loss of hearing was supposed to happen, and there's a damn good reason for it?

Hmmm? But you're not telling her everything and—

Okay, I get it. We have to take this slow with her, considering what a perfectionist she is and all. What's that? Yeah, I know. She has to learn to deal with difficulty and not become paralyzed with fear. And I've gotta tell you, she has a ways to go before she gets the lesson because right now she's absolutely, completely, and totally terrified.

I can't push her just a teensy bit? Because, you know sometimes I can actually get her attention that way. What's that? I've done enough for now? Are you really, really sure?

So, do you think she's ever going to reach the point where she gets all this? I mean, she has all the pieces in place to grow. She has Daddy and you and, of course, moi.

What's that? Of course I know French. At least, as much as she knows.

Okay, I'll be cool. I'll back away and let her get used to the deaf thing. We'll just hope she learns to overcome her fear in the process. But she can be so slow. It's a damned good thing I'm a very patient, evolved being.

I was stunned. And Anita's—and apparently, Kalli's—humor about my little dog's deafness did nothing to mollify my distress. If anything, their lighthearted attitude angered me.

I spent the day drifting from hour to hour, as if in a waking nightmare. Upon Marc's return home from work, I had barely let him walk through the door before I pounced on him, relaying the day's events in excruciating detail.

He studied me for a long moment without saying a word, then shifted to stare at Kalli. I could have sworn the little bugger winked at him.

"You really think this is funny?" I growled at her.

Marc looked at me in shock. "What? I don't think this is funny."

"I'm not talking to you." Suddenly, the day's high drama got the better of me, and I dissolved into tears. I could almost hear Kalli complain about my overreaction and how I was being silly.

"Cut it out," I snapped at her through my tears.

"Okay, now you're freaking me out," said Marc, eyeing me with obvious concern.

I attacked the tissue box in the kitchen, pulling out tissues with fierce yanks. "I'm"—*yank*—"not"—*yank*—"talking"—*yank*—"to you!"

I stalked back into the family room and dropped onto the couch, staring at the crackling fire in the stone fireplace. My eyes drifted to Kalli, who was snuggling in her bed with a contented sigh.

Marc walked over to stand behind her. In an excited voice that never failed to rouse her, he said, "Hey, Kalli! Let's get a treat, honey. Do you want a treat?"

She didn't move a muscle as she began to snore.

Marc's shock was palpable. "Good God," he breathed.

"Exactly." My grim tone sounded funereal, even to me. I reminded him about her lack of reaction to the neighbor dogs.

"You're right. She'd never ignore those yappy things unless…"

"…unless she couldn't hear them," I finished for him.

We stared at our dog, lapsing into a sad silence only punctuated by Kalli's wheezy snores. Suddenly, Marc started laughing.

I glared at him in shock. "You said you didn't think this was funny," I snapped.

He shook his head. "You have to look at this from her perspective. What did Anita say? That Kalli wasn't the least bit upset about this? I'll say! Just look at her." He gestured toward our sleeping canine, who had shifted in her bed until her body from head to mid-tummy draped off the green velvet and onto the carpeting. She'd twisted around so the portion of her body on the rug faced the ceiling, while the rest of her was still in the bed curled on one side. We called this her "forward half-twist" position…one of her favorites.

"Does that look like a distressed dog to you?"

I struggled with annoyance at Marc's lightheartedness and forced myself to calm down. "Okay, okay. You're right."

"Honey?"

His gentle voice grabbed my attention. "What?"

"You're into life lessons, right? Perhaps this is one."

"Crappy lesson."

"Yeah, well, I'd have to agree there. But if you step away so you can look at the big picture, I think Kalli is teaching us how to live with grace and acceptance when things go wrong. You know?"

"No, I don't know." Anger fired in my gut once again, and I launched from the couch to pace the floor. "What I *do* know is this sucks."

"Hey, if the one affected isn't getting upset, why on earth are you?"

That shut me up. I wanted to protest, but my sense of fair play stopped me in my tracks. Instead, I marched into the kitchen to begin dinner, grumbling, "Whatever."

Events of the next few weeks unfolded as one grand lesson, just as Marc and Anita had suggested. Kalli sailed through her days with her normal merriment, tinged with a hint of self-satisfied gloating. Okay, so maybe the gloating part was my imagination, but I was *sure* I saw a devilish glint in her eyes I'd never noticed before. And on occasion, she'd raise her eyebrows at me in a sardonic way that told me she was having the time of her life.

Our daily walk habits changed with my new reluctance to allow Kalli off-leash in any but the safest environments. The fact that she couldn't hear if I had to call her in to me had made me cautious. And obviously, the lack of dialogue between Kalli and our yappy neighbor dogs continued. Kalli's non-response still chilled me, but then I'd watch her follow the trail of an animal scent in our meadow with pure joy, and I'd realize all was right in the world. This was a dog who loved her life. The inability to hear sounds seemed to make no difference at all to her.

Other, more profound behaviors shifted…primarily with me. I had spent years chattering to my little girl. While on the surface, I had always adopted the "party line" that she probably didn't understand a word I said, on a more profound level, I'd suspected she had comprehend my conversation. After learning about the process animal communicators used to work with her, I became convinced she "got" me as I spoke to her. Indeed, the feedback I received from her through Anita and others confirmed this.

So, now I was placed in the odd position of talking to her and being forced to *have faith* she really did "hear" me on another level…one of energy. If I didn't believe this, I'd have no choice but to consider *all* lines of interaction—except visual—closed to us. And that I couldn't accept.

I continued to talk to her, just as I always had. However, now, that element of faith grew within me. In my most objective moments, I thanked the Universe for the gift Kalli was giving me. After all, if it hadn't been for her deafness, I never would have been pushed to step beyond my comfort zone.

At those times, Anita's comment about Kalli being a Master Teacher returned to me. While I knew in my heart Kalli had been teaching us for years, this latest lesson had to be the most dramatic scenario we had ever encountered. The fact that everyone in the household was evolving exponentially because of it only affirmed Kalli's special role in our lives.

Our lessons didn't end with her deafness. And the first hint of the next challenge occurred at a gas station, of all places.

I had pulled into the place to fill up the car's tank after Kalli and I had finished a long hike through woods at a nearby open space park.

As I went about my business, I rolled down the rear windows so Kalli could stick her head out and sniff the world.

The station and its tiny store constructed of rough-hewn logs—appropriately called the "Little Log Cabin"—crouched deep in the foothills off US 285 near our home. The proprietor, a dog lover whom Kalli and I often met on our walks, poked her head out the store window when she saw us parked by the pump. A minute later, she was standing at the car, feeding Kalli a biscuit.

As Kalli munched, Ella stroked her head, commenting on her glistening fur shining in the sunlight. "So, how long has she had cataracts? Probably not long, right?" Ella asked in a casual tone.

"Excuse me?" I stared at the woman.

"Yeah, you can see them in the sun if she turns her head a certain way…that cloudiness in her eyes? It's not real obvious, but there's no

doubt. That's the beginning of cataracts."

I froze. On the heels of Kalli's deafness, I hit an emotional wall as the word "blind" attacked me. Kalli, of course, was having the time of her life munching on Ella's

biscuits.

I don't remember driving the short distance to the house, nor any of the small details that transitioned Kalli and me from the car to the family room. But a few minutes later, I was staring at Kalli as she settled into her bed by the fireplace as if nothing was amiss.

"How can you be so frigging calm?" I finally exploded at her. "Cataracts? Really, Kalli?"

She opened one eye, looked at me and sighed, then closed it again. Within a minute, she'd nestled deeper in her bed with a yawn.

Oh, geesh, Mom. I knew you were going to get all upset on me, but I didn't think it would be THIS bad. I figured after the deafness thing, you'd learned to deal better than this.

Siiiiiiiigh. Okay, for the record, I'm not crazy about having cataracts myself. I didn't plan it like the deafness, it just happened to me. But being the evolved soul I am, I understand all things happen for a reason, so I'm going to accept the situation with my usual grace and style. As for you—

Hmmm. You do have a bit of style, but I'm not sure about grace. You have a long way to go before you can handle stuff like this with grace.

Well, there you have it. Another lesson giving you the opportunity to continue learning and growing.

Hey, I'm putting myself out, here. The least you can do is take this to heart and chill just the teensiest bit. For me. Come on, Mom, you can do it.

Chill.

I was so upset, I didn't even have the heart to call Anita and ask her for the details of this most recent distressing news. I didn't need to. Ella had pointed out the subtle cloudiness blanketing Kalli's eyes. I knew what that meant.

My sense of time distorted as I sat on the couch staring at Kalli.

At some point during the afternoon, a tiny seed of determination planted itself in my heart. And with it came the realization that nutritional supplements could be given to Kalli that would, at the very least, slow down the progression of her cataracts.

I called Kay, the queen of natural solutions to medical issues. As fate would have it, she was just "coming up the hill" from Denver toward her home in the mountains and was approaching the turnoff to our house. Minutes later, she walked into the front hall with her signature "Helllooooo." She hadn't rung our doorbell or knocked in years. Kay was a member of the family.

I raced to her and hung on for dear life.

Kay, to her credit, took my drama in stride. "Uh, what's up?"

By now, I had started crying and couldn't stop.

With calm and patience, Kay waited until my sobs had degenerated to sighs, then made us a pot of tea. "Kalli looks fine to me, Laura." She talked as she worked. "Why the distress?"

"Cataracts." It was the only word I could verbalize at the moment.

"Really?" Kay handed me a steaming mug of Darjeeling. "What makes you say so?"

I told Kay about my visit to the Little Log Cabin. By the time I finished, I was crying again, and she was studying Kalli with a frown.

"Besides which, I saw the cloudiness myself, Kay." I dragged my eyes away from Kalli and back to my friend. "Why would she elect to go through this? Especially after the deafness?"

"Knowing Kalli, she has a damned good reason." Kay shrugged and added in a gentle voice, "It's all about the lessons, Laura. You know that."

"I wish I didn't," I ground out through gritted teeth. Truth was, I was furious at my little dog. I wasn't proud of that reaction, but I'm only human.

Kalli had roused herself by this time. Spying Kay curled into the armchair by the fire, she wiggled her way over to say hello.

Kay reached down to give her a back rub. "What are you doing to your mom, Kalli? Huh? Wasn't the deafness enough?"

Kalli wiggled her butt harder. "Okay, little girl." Kay sighed. "Let's take a look at those eyes of yours." She led Kalli to the full-length windows by the patio door and positioned her facing the sunlight.

I held my breath, waiting for Kay's words, hoping Ella and I were imagining things.

"Yup. Definitely the start of cataracts." Kay straightened and smiled sadly. "But, the good news is we can slow down the progression.

With any luck, she'll live a long life and experience only slight dimming of her sight."

Hope jumped in my gut. "Really?"

"There's a type of eye drop that has proven to be really great at bolstering the eyes. It's expensive, though."

"I don't care. Give me the name of it. We'll pay any price."

"And blueberry extract. See if you can mix it in her food and get her to eat it that way. Bilberry, too." Kay paused. "I'll make you a list. Most of the stuff you can purchase at any natural food store."

I had pulled out a pad of paper and was busy taking notes. Before Kay left, I had a page filled with my scrawls…each word brimming with optimism.

Marc and I launched a regimen with Kalli that would have made the most hardcore nutritionist proud. At the center of the routine was the precious eye drop liquid. After a few attempts that saw me squirting the stuff everywhere but in Kalli's eyes, I figured out that if I backed Kalli up against me and I sat on the floor with legs spread, she couldn't escape the drops. She wasn't thrilled with the process, but she didn't fight, either. I considered this a significant success.

Events moved along without any change in our Kalli routine until early one winter morning—a year after that frigid January day when I'd discovered my dog's deafness. This time, the change in routine took a different form than it had then. I noticed that rather than bolting out the front door into the pre-dawn shadows, Kalli hesitated on the threshold. Once I'd flipped on the porch light, she walked across the deck surface carefully. Over the next few days, I watched her move deliberately whenever she was in low-light situations. I tried to ignore my thought that she was acting like a little old lady, feeling her way along.

"Well, honey, she's getting older," Anita said in response to my telephone call. "I think you forget, sometimes, she's in her early seventies in people-years. There's nothing wrong with her slowing down. We all get older, Laura. It's part of the natural cycle of things. The trick is to take it in stride and enjoy every moment of life."

I glanced at Kalli, who sprawled across my feet under my desk. The notion of her becoming an old dog had never occurred to me before.

"Laura, do you remember when you and Marc went to Breckenridge a few months ago and I watched Kalli for you?"

"Of course."

"Well, I got an earful from her over those few days."

"You never said anything."

"It wasn't time to tell you."

I stifled annoyance. "So tell me now."

"Kalli showed me a treadmill, moving at a fast clip. You were striding on it, dragging her behind you."

"Dragging—"

"Nothing abusive. The image wasn't meant to say you were intentionally hurting Kalli. There's more."

"Go on."

"Well, there you and Kalli were, on the treadmill as it revved. Then, it abruptly stopped, throwing both you and Kalli off balance." Anita paused, then added in a softer voice, "At first, I wasn't sure what this shift from moving to stopping meant, but Kalli clarified it for me the next morning. You know how you've been carrying Kalli down the stairs from the bedroom ever since her neck injury?"

"Yes."

"Well, she hates the fact that you won't let her go down that stairway to the main floor on her own. She told me so."

My mind flashed on Kalli's patented, controlled fall that had always characterized her descent on stairs when she was left to her own devices.

Anita went on. "It was really quite extraordinary, the way she told me."

"Okaaaay."

"That morning, as we made our way down the stairs, Kalli in my arms, she spoke very loudly in my head and with amazing distinctness. It probably took quite a bit of energy for her to do that. Anyway, she said, 'I hate this.' Really, Laura, I don't think you know how unusual it is to have an animal speak as clearly as that."

"Well, we know she's a special dog." My thoughts were spinning as I processed what Anita was saying. "I'm assuming she was referring to being carried down the stairs?"

"Yes, indeed."

"But, she has difficulty on those steps. Especially now that her eyesight has dimmed."

Anita sighed. "You're not understanding the message. Go back to the treadmill. Did it move at a constant rate?"

"No."

"So, there was a jerking thing going on, right? It was either too fast or not moving at all."

I caught myself nodding to the phone receiver. "It went from one extreme to the other."

"Exactly!"

I looked down to see that Kalli, who had been sleeping, was now staring at me. "You're unbelievable," I muttered to her.

"Honey, she knows the stairs. She can see them in her head." Anita paused. "You walk her around the outside of the house when you're going down to the lower level, right?"

"Right."

"So, we're only talking about her managing one set of steps from the top floor. Trust her with them."

My mind filled with images of Kalli tumbling down steps she could no longer see clearly. And aggravating her bad disc in the process.

Anita's quiet voice drifted across my mind's eye. "You're still bouncing from one extreme to the other in your head. Consider the message behind the jerking treadmill." Anita was nothing if not patient.

"What are you suggesting?"

"A midcourse correction. Something that will keep Kalli safe, but still allow her to take those steps on her own. Keep her harness and leash in the bedroom. Put them on her after you've let her out of the crate in the morning. That way, if she starts to stumble, you can hold her in place long enough to stabilize her. But, otherwise, she's in control of her own situation. What do you think?"

"But her neck…"

A *harrumph* shifted my attention back to Kalli. She had now fixed me with one of her famous glares.

Geesh, Mom. It's not rocket science. Although I have to disagree with Grandma. I don't even need the leash and harness thing. They really cramp my style, and you know how I hate that! But if it'll make you feel better, I'll humor you. One more time.

Bottom line is you're so scared something will happen to me, you're suffocating me and affecting…hmmm. What do you humans call it? Oh, yeah. My quality of life. And really, you should know better than to do that after all these years.

If I fall on the stairs, then I fall. Big deal. It's better than being strangled by your fear. Let my experience teach you that stuff happens and it's okay. It's okay I'm going blind. It's okay I'm deaf. The point is to find fun. And really, you can always find fun, Mom. You just have to know where to look.

"In a perfect world, you'd continue carrying her down the stairs.

I get that," said Anita. "But you have to look at a picture bigger than just Kalli's neck."

"Her happiness is important, too. Is that what you're telling me?"

Kalli's soft *woof* coincided with Anita saying, "That's it exactly. You're beginning to see the larger picture, getting a sense of the balance this situation is begging for. Very good."

Suddenly, images of the cat we'd owned years before hit me between the eyes. "Poor Bregen." I sighed.

Anita paused, and I knew she was "listening" to her Guides. "Yes, you forced the issue with that animal, didn't you?"

"And made her miserable in the process."

At the end of her life, Bregen suffered from kidney failure. Our vet recommended we hydrate her every day. Unfortunately, we never could get the hang of inserting the needle necessary for the IV, so I would stuff her into her crate and drag her to the clinic each morning. She hated every minute of it. But because I believed the hydration was in her best interests, I ignored the emotional misery she suffered. That combined with forcing her to eat special food she absolutely detested meant her last days were miserable.

Now, I realized I'd sabotaged her quality of life in exchange for having a few more months with her.

"I was selfish and shortsighted," I muttered under my breath. A bump against my knee broke my mental self-flagellation. Kalli nudged my leg with her nose, glaring at me as she did so. I didn't need a communicator to know she was telling me to cut it out.

"Listen to Kalli," Anita said. "She's exactly right. Oh, and by the way, Bregen understood you were taking those actions at the end of her life because you genuinely thought they were in her best interests. There's no blame there."

"Those were the lessons she was teaching me."

"That's right."

"Too bad I learned them way too late."

Anita sighed. "What's too late? The important thing is you're learning them. If you continue to beat yourself up, you're betraying her wisdom."

Really, Mom. Listen to Anita, for pity's sake. Look, when we teach our humans their lessons, all we can do is hope they "get it" eventually. There's no rule or grading scale. Actually, Bregen is pretty thrilled right now because you were able to look back and see her situation in a different way. You've had a...a...what have I heard it called? Oh, yeah. A shift in perception. And that's totally cool.

So, take a deep breath and relax. Puleeeease? Bregen's happy. I'm happy. And hey...you should be happy, too.

FRAIL

Thus began a new—and final—phase of Kalli's physical life. Her eyesight dimmed progressively over the next year. Marc and I noticed subtle changes as Kalli slowed her pace and maneuvered around her world with increasing care.

"So, how do we handle this?" I turned to Marc one Saturday morning as we watched Kalli bump into the wall of the hallway leading from the front door to the kitchen. She quickly collected herself, corrected her course, and continued as if nothing had happened. "I'm afraid she's going to hurt herself at this rate."

"Give her space." He held up a hand to stifle my protest. "I know. It seems counterintuitive, but look who we're dealing with here. The last thing Kalli wants is for us to get in her way. Hovering would create a hell far worse than her loss of hearing and sight."

"Yeah, I know you're right." I paused, my thoughts tumbling around this latest predicament with our dog. Clearly, she was adjusting to her situation far more gracefully than I was. So what else was new?

No kidding, Mom. I got this whole blindness thing down pat. You have some serious work to do, however.

I mean, am I thrilled with my useless eyes? Nope. Grandma Anita asked me what I wanted Auntie Kay to work on during my last adjustment, and I told her, in so uncertain terms, I wanted my sight back. Siiiiigh. I know that made Grandma sad, and that wasn't what I wanted at all, you understand. I was just being honest. I keep forgetting you humans don't handle pure honesty very well. And it's easy to forget with Grandma because she deals with unvarnished truth so much better than the rest of you. Still, she was upset and felt the need to explain to me that my eyes can't be fixed.

I mean, I knew that, for pity's sake. I guess I thought maybe if I asked...

Anyway, I'm not one to wallow, that I can tell you. And I'm trying to teach you not to wallow, too.

I don't mean to be harsh with you. I know your lessons can really hang you up, and the fact that you're willing to learn them says a lot of really great stuff about you. It's just frustrating to watch you struggle.

I took a deep breath, resolving to look at Kalli's situation in a different light. So, what was positive about Kalli's blindness? My good intentions slammed into a mental stone wall. Geesh, how could I possibly find anything positive about losing one's sight?

You're almost there, Mom. Keep at it.

Fact is, there is something really cool about what happened to me. Think... Allow yourself to be absorbed by this spaniel mind meld.

Think... Think...

Suddenly, I realized Kalli had been fortunate to lose her sight gradually, over time. I verbalized this thought to Marc, adding, "So, Kalli's had a chance to adjust to the increasing limitation and figure out how to maneuver in spite of it." I shuddered, remembering stories

I'd heard from folks whose dogs had gone blind overnight. The shock for both humans and canines had been extreme.

Marc nodded toward our dog, who had sailed over to her bed by the fireplace as if she had 20/20 sight to guide her there. She settled into the bed, mashing one of the pillows with her muzzle before she dropped her head onto the spot with a "harrumph!"

"I think you're absolutely right about Kalli being given the opportunity to ease into her blindness. I mean, do you see her struggling at all?"

In fact, I didn't. The same indomitable Kalli spirit propelled her through her days. And the Kalli style? That arrogant *look at me, I know better than anyone else* thing she'd always had about her? It was still there, evident in the cocky way she maneuvered around her house. The only adjustments that seemed necessary now were my attitude and Kalli's environment to accommodate her limited senses.

I began wandering through the first floor of our house, looking around me with new eyes. Where were the danger spots for Kalli? How much freedom could we give her and still keep her safe? A plan began to emerge.

"The only real issue on this floor is the stairway going to the lower level," I told Marc, eyeing the steps as if they'd become a mortal enemy. "So, if we gated off this doorway…"

"Then she'd be fine on this floor," Marc said in my ear as he stood behind me. "She's smart, Laura. She knows what her limitations are. And she's learning to get around by using her muzzle to feel the walls and furniture legs. Now we just need to keep the floor clear of clutter."

I looked over to the family room where Kalli lay in her bed "watching" us. The morning sunlight streamed through the glass of the nearby patio door, illuminating the milky surface of her eyes. "If only we could operate on those blasted cataracts." I spit out the words through gritted teeth.

"Considering how much she hates to be messed with?" Marc shook his head. "Subjecting her to the stress of an operation would be cruel, honey. Especially at her age."

Really, you two? You're really going to feel sorry for me just because I can't see? Geesh. Have you guys learned nothing from me after all these years?

Please stop the "poor us" thing. Do you see me lying in a corner and having a pity party? Of course you don't. Hell, I can still smell. And my treats are as tasty as ever. Believe me, food is really the most important thing of all. Always has been.

I'm going to darn well continue enjoying myself, despite these stupid eyes. There's a lot of living yet to do. And cookies to eat...

Speaking of which, how about my breakfast, Mom? A dog could starve around here. You think you'd have mercy on this pathetic old blind mutt. Tee...hee...

As the weeks passed, our lives settled into a new pattern with Kalli. And I began to treasure the Kalli-friendly layout of our yard and house.

Getting outside for potty trips was a breeze for her. She only had two steps to navigate from the doorway to the yard. Once in the yard, an expanse of level pavement in front of the house spread before her. Kalli didn't have to contend with uneven, sloping ground if she didn't want to.

Still, I worried about her footing when we were outside, even though I guided her at the other end of the leash. Now and then, I'd catch her glaring at me with her sightless eyes if I hovered too closely.

Yeah, I know what you're thinking. But I'm not an invalid. I really do know what I'm doing...in more ways than one.

Look, you have to stop treating me like I'm on death's doorstep. I'm still here, going strong. Just a little bit slower than I used to be. Remember, I've lived in this house and yard for nine years, and I only lost my sight recently. I know where everything is, as long as you don't go moving stuff around, of course.

So chill. Please? You're distracting me from this lovely pile of fox poop. And I can tell you, the animal that dumped this had an amazing day, if my nose is any judge.

Navigating indoors was also easy for Kalli thanks to the circular layout of the main floor. In the mornings, she still found her way down the stairs from the bedroom on her own steam, secure in her harness and leash. Once on the first floor, Kalli was "undressed" so she could move without restraints of any kind. She'd march down the hallway to where it ended by her food dish in the kitchen and await her breakfast. After eating her meal, she'd enter the family room that opened before her and settle in her bed. If she was in the mood to wander, she'd feel her way along the wall that separated the kitchen from the breakfast nook, then meander into the dining room, step around the couch in the living room, and head back to the entranceway.

I moved my work space from my lower level office to the breakfast nook so I could be with Kalli throughout the day as she settled into life on the main floor.

When Marc and I left Kalli alone in the house, we placed a gate in the dining room entrance and another one midway down the hall running between the front door and kitchen. This gave Kalli access to her food and water in the kitchen, her bed in the family room, and the breakfast nook—plenty of room to wander and still be safe.

Being the brilliant dog she was, Kalli quickly became accustomed to the placement of the gates. We'd catch her pause in the spot where they could be, nose forward to test the space for their presence, then either correct course if they were up, or move ahead with confidence if the way was clear.

Regardless of our careful planning, accidents were inevitable. One morning, Kalli followed Marc on his heels as he headed for the stairway to the lower level. He removed the gate from the top step so he could descend and, deep in conversation with me, wasn't quick enough replacing it. Kalli scooted around him and promptly fell down the first flight to the landing.

I shrieked and started after her.

To my amazement, she picked herself up and shook off the fall as if nothing had happened. Then she stood in place on the landing, waiting to be rescued. She was the picture of calm.

I paused, processing what I was seeing, struck by how relaxed the whole event had been. What could have been a disaster was, in reality, a casual "oops" moment.

As if Kalli had entered my head, I heard the words:

Yeah, I'm cool and calm. I stayed loose and didn't hassle the fall as it was happening. If I'd been tense? I'd have been screwed...and injured. As it is, I'm fine!

I joined her on the landing, eyeing her with suspicion. "Am I going crazy or are you talking to me?"

Oh, man! Give me a loaded question, will you. Now, how am I supposed to answer that, for pity's sake?

Ummm. Yeah, you are kinda crazy. But were you aware of my talking to you? You bet! And you did a really good job of listening, too...for someone as tight and controlled as you are. Of course, I did make an extra effort to reach you. And that takes a lot of energy. I'm exhausted.

Do you think you could guide me up the stairs so I can take a nap in my nice, safe, cushy bed?

Very good. That's a good human.

After I'd gotten Kalli back to the main floor, I watched with eagle eyes as she walked down the hall, alert to any hint of limping or discomfort resulting from her tumble. But I didn't detect a bit of difference in her movement. She was, indeed, fine.

Still, I was relieved when Kay arrived for her regular appointment with Kalli the next day. It didn't hurt to have a professional check out my little dog, just in case.

"You know she's doing great." Kay's eyes followed Kalli as her patient bumped into the refrigerator.

I winced at the sight, in spite of myself. "It hurts every time I see her run into something like that."

Kay swung her attention back to me and smiled slightly. "I know. And that's to be expected. You're her mom, after all. But really, I've seen dogs who are blind and deaf just shut down. They give up on life and usually die far sooner than they would have otherwise. But this one?" She cocked her head toward the spaniel who pranced slowly toward her.

Kay arrested Kalli's progress by cupping the gorgeous muzzle between her hands. "This one is still enjoying herself. It's her spirit that counts. And I'd say that spirit is as lively as ever, just expressing itself differently than it used to."

I sighed. "I'm sure you're right. But, Kay, she's spending so much time sleeping. Is that normal?"

"Laura, she's fourteen! And getting around is taking more out of her than it used to. Give her a break."

"You and Kalli are in league, aren't you?" I laughed, feeling my tension melt under the influence of Kay's calm and Kalli's certainty.

"We're just able to see the situation without your emotions, that's all." Kay paused and stared at me for a long moment. "I know I'm probably telling you something you already know, Laura, but when Kalli's ready to leave you, she'll let you know. Believe me, all dogs communicate that very clearly. And this one?" Kay chuckled. "She's the ultimate communicator. There won't be any question in your mind."

"Until then, I should treasure the time I have with her," I finished.

"Exactly."

Another aspect of Kalli's life remained the same despite her sensory losses. She was still the consummate teacher. We had hired a massage therapist to come to the house, rather than stressing Kalli by placing her in a shop environment. It didn't take long before Piper began learning lessons from her client.

One day, Piper arrived at the house and began her work, only to break off. From the other room, I heard her say, "Kalli, what's the problem?" I walked into the living room where Piper sat cross-legged on the floor. Kalli sprawled a short distance away, her back to Piper.

"What's going on?" I asked the therapist.

Piper shook her head. "I don't know. She won't settle down for me."

Time for the services of the family's resident psychic.

"Picking up anything?" I asked Anita over the phone a few minutes later.

Silence descended as Anita tuned in to Kalli. "Well, Kalli is definitely in a snit over something. Let me talk to Piper."

I handed over the phone and tried to get a sense of the conversation as I listened to Piper's responses to Anita's questions. A few minutes later, Piper disconnected the call and flashed me a rueful smile. "Well, I guess your dog told me!"

"What?"

"When I showed up this morning, I was worried about my dog. Kalli refused to let me touch her as long as my attention was elsewhere." Piper turned to Kalli. "I promise I'll focus on you and you alone. Can we get to work now?"

As if on cue, Kalli stood and turned toward Piper, then stretched out on the carpet in front of her.

Piper laughed. "So, all is well now, little girl? You've made your point?"

Indeed, that did seem to be the case as Kalli settled into her massage as if she didn't have a care in the world. On subsequent visits, Piper's emotional state became obvious to all just by observing Kalli's reaction to her. While my dog never refused her ministrations again, Kalli did use subtle cues to make certain Piper was fully present during each session.

"Are you familiar with the author Jon Kabat-Zinn?" Piper asked me one day.

I shook my head. "Why?"

"He's the developer of a process known as MBSR."

"Which stands for…?"

"Mindfulness-Based Stress Reduction. I've been very interested in his healing techniques ever since I saw him on a PBS show with Bill Moyers. His concept focuses on being alive in the moment…fully aware of every aspect of now…smells, sounds, sights. We find true peace when we let the past and future go and just…be."

"Sounds wonderful."

"Well, let me just say your dog is a better teacher of this concept than any human I've ever met. And believe me, I've been to tons of seminars and weekend sessions. Kalli simply refuses to let me be anything but in the moment. Once my thoughts start to stray during a massage, she shuts down on me. I'm telling you, the shift in my process has been huge since I started working with her. I'm much more focused on my clients, thanks to her."

I looked over to see Kalli's face turned toward us. I could have sworn I saw a sly grin spread across her face.

Hey, the woman needs to pay attention. What can I say? I was just helping in her journey. And what a load she has to carry. Quite the lifetime she's chosen this time around. She's really gifted and was born to be a healer. But she gets in her own way. Of course, she won't after I'm finished with her.

Trust me, Mom, you don't need eyes and ears to get all this. In fact, sometimes it helps to listen inside when you can't hear and see in the conventional sense. And remember, I ain't dead yet. I still have stuff to do before I leave this pathetic body of mine.

I stared at her, knowing she was in my head, but I couldn't get a handle on her words. Suddenly, I knew intuitively if I just stopped trying so hard, her message would come to me. I drew a deep breath, then exhaled. Immediately, a sense of well-being swept over me. Everything was just as it should be.

One night, months after Kalli's sight had disappeared, I found myself tossing and turning in bed. Now, I've had my share of sleepless nights over the years, but on this occasion, the sensation was unique. It was as if a very tangible, bricks-and-mortar wall had sprung up between me and sleep. Powerless to breach it, I suffered through the night wide-eyed and miserable.

I stumbled through the next day, confident I'd sleep like a rock that night. After all, I was exhausted, right? Sleep was a sure thing. But the next night was a repeat of the first one.

By the end of the third night without a second of shuteye, I proclaimed myself an official basket case. Deprivation had left me shaky and caught in the hell of an unrelenting anxiety attack. It worsened as the hours passed.

The fourth night found me prowling through the house, muttering. I lurched through the bedroom, glaring at Marc in peaceful slumber on the bed and Kalli snoring in her crate. How dare they while away the nocturnal hours like that? It wasn't fair. And I was jealous. No, I was beyond jealous, I was furious at them.

I was losing my mind.

Only after obtaining a prescription for a strong sleep aid and a few nights of solid rest did I start to calm down. With a bit of reason returning to my feverish brain, I reflected on what had happened over the course of the week. What the hell?

I found myself staring at Kalli a few days after I'd regained some semblance of mental equilibrium. Her head turned in my direction and for a moment, our eyes met.

No. No, that wasn't possible. She had no ability to focus. And yet, those orbs of hers suddenly seemed alive, active. Vital.

Keep trying to reach me, Mom. That's right. Because there's an important lesson for you to pick up, right now.

Come on. You can do it.

Okay, so you're still too fuzzy to hear me. Let's see if I can figure out another way to get through to you.

Suddenly, Anita's words from years earlier reverberated through my head. I remembered how she told me about the way dogs processed for us. How they took our garbage energy and cleared it away so we could use our resources more productively.

So, throughout all these years, Kalli had been processing for Marc and me. But, with her advancing age and increasingly frail condition, what would happen if she suddenly stopped? If she had no more energy available to expend on her humans?

Then it would feel as if a wall had gone up, blocking my ability to relax and…sleep.

Oh… my…God.

As I continued staring at Kalli, I knew I'd figured out the mystery of my sleepless nights. My little girl was marshalling her reserves.

Relief washed over me. And sadness, too. At least I was no longer afraid I was going insane. But understanding Kalli's situation brought in sharp relief the ramifications of her advancing age.

I struggled to place this latest insight into a healthy perspective. But balance stayed just beyond my reach as Marc and I watched Kalli slip away from us bit by bit each day. As the months passed, she began to sleep more and more.

When asked about this, Anita talked to me in soothing tones. "She's spending time on the Other Side, Laura. There's nothing wrong with this, by the way. It's very normal. She's preparing, that's all."

"That's all?"

"I know it's hard, honey. And I'm being affected, too. I haven't heard from her at all lately."

"So, what does that mean?"

"That she's rationing her strength, using it when she needs it and staying low-key when she doesn't."

"I miss her. I miss going on walks with her and…" My throat closed on me as I choked back a sob. A few months earlier, I'd realized the daily walk was stressing her…she'd been straining to keep up with me. With the joy gone, and Kalli's physicality unable to handle the experience comfortably, there had been no reason to continue the outings with her. In a desperate attempt to maintain some sense of balance in my life, and instinctively knowing I had to embrace the transition facing me, I'd begun to walk alone, purposely choosing places I'd been with Kalli. It was beyond difficult.

"But she's still with you. And when you come back to the house from a hike, she's waiting for you and bugging you for treats. Honey, she's trying to ease you into the changes."

But the changes were anything but easy, the latest of which was Kalli's increasing inability to control her bladder and bowels. I purchased incontinence pads and covered the family room rug with them. They made the clean-up so much easier. Between them and getting Kalli outside frequently, we minimized the disruption brought about by the reversal of Kalli's housetraining.

We also limited the amount of time we left her alone. A maximum of five hours away from the house soon became four hours, then three, two, and finally one. In short, our lives now revolved around Kalli in a very different way than they used to.

As the months went by, Marc and I couldn't help but wonder how much longer she would be with us.

TRANSITION

During the last year of Kalli's life, Marc and I accepted each day we spent with her as a gift. At times, it proved to be a painful gift.

The final shift in our routine occurred during the early hours of an August morning. A sound had awakened me. I lay in bed trying to fight through layers of drowsiness to identify it. A minute later, I heard Kalli panting in her crate by the bed.

Flicking on the light, I looked over to see her pacing within the limits of her kennel. Frantic, she staggered, moving as fast as she could, her sightless eyes unable to save her from the bumpers as her body careened against the upholstered-covered walls.

I glanced at the clock as I grabbed the crate door handle and yanked. It was three o'clock.

She seemed to sense me, and her pace quickened. I started to talk to her, then stopped. She couldn't hear me, and given her panicked state, she probably wasn't tuning in to me on an energetic level, either.

A few minutes later, I'd eased her downstairs and outside to potty. Then I guided her to her bed in the family room, and turned on the television and espresso machine.

That was the last night Kalli spent in her crate, ending fourteen years of a familiar pattern. While Marc and I placed her in the kennel at bedtime on subsequent evenings, she refused to settle. The safest thing we could do for her was to let her sleep downstairs in her bed by the fireplace.

We established overnight roaming territory with the baby gates…a delicate balance between giving her enough room to stretch her legs so she wouldn't feel constricted, and limiting her area to keep her safe without our constant supervision.

Marc and I never rested comfortably from that point on. At first, we spent our nights up in the bedroom, barely breathing, always alert to any sound coming from downstairs, making frequent trips to check on her. Eventually, we alternated sleeping on the family room couch so one of us could be near her throughout the night.

We shifted our morning potty duty from six o'clock to four. But we were never early enough, nor diligent enough, to spare Kalli the humiliation of soiling one of the many incontinence pads we'd spread across the carpet.

Kay scolded me when I berated myself over this. "Don't go there, Laura. You can't spend every waking moment hovering over her. And she wouldn't want you to."

Kay drew some of Kalli's blood for tests. I had wrestled with myself over whether or not to have her do this procedure, loath to cause Kalli more discomfort. But I wanted to understand what was going on in my dog's body.

At her next visit, Kay informed us the tests showed lymphoblastic leukemia and anemia. Kalli's red cell count was less than fifteen percent of normal. Her kidney function had dropped to less than twenty percent.

Kay answered my silent question. "Forget the clinical indicators. She'll tell you when it's time. You'll know."

One day a few weeks later, Kalli refused to eat. Kalli. The dog who would do anything for a treat…refused…to…eat.

The next morning, at the crack of dawn, I awoke from the family room couch to find all the cotton floor pads soiled. Kalli stood in the middle of the mess, panting and trembling.

At eight o'clock, I called Anita. Pain welled up in my throat until I could barely draw breath. "This is it," I rasped into the phone.

"Yes, honey." Anita's gentle voice stabbed through the bit of composure I had left.

I disconnected her call, punched Kay's number, and told her we needed her at the house.

"I won't ask if you're sure," came Kay's quiet response. "I'll be there within the hour."

Marc and I replaced the white pads, started a load of soiled cotton in the washer, then stared at one another for long moments. The shock of what was about to happen crept over me. Icy needles of hysteria threatened to take over.

I shook them off and pulled myself to my feet. "I'm taking her out." *One last time.*

"Do you really think—" Marc broke off as he studied my face. Silently, he fell in step behind me.

With a steadying hand along Kalli's side, I guided her down the hall to the front door. My fingers trembled as I put her in the harness and hooked the leash to it.

The last time. The last time.

The drumbeat flooded my head. Tears filled my eyes. By the time I had walked Kalli off the porch and onto the pavement in front of the house, I was sobbing.

I ignored the stream of tears dripping across my little girl's back as we walked the circuit of the driveway. At one point, Kalli stopped and piddled a tiny bit. Then she trundled toward the house, her unerring instincts guiding her back to bed.

I dried my tears and sank onto the couch. My eyes sought out Marc's. No words were necessary. We'd reached the end of a journey with Kalli. It was time to accept it, honor her life, and help her transition.

When I heard Kay open the front door, the tears started again. For long moments, she and I stood in the hall, arms wrapped around each other. I sobbed into her shoulder, then broke away.

She nodded briskly and walked toward Kalli, who was lying on the family room floor by Marc's chair. Sitting next to her, Kay murmured, "Well, lovely lady. I guess you told us, didn't you?" For several moments, she stroked Kalli's back, whispering to her. Then she dried her tears and reached for her medical bag.

Marc and I joined her on the floor. The three of us surrounded

Kalli.

The process that took Kalli's body away from us remains a blur. I remember Kalli struggling a bit at one point and Kay quieting her gently. Within minutes, her breathing stopped and her body stilled.

I froze, staring down at the lifeless form. Where was Kalli?

Oh, puleeeeeeeeze! You're going to make a big deal out of this, aren't you?

I jerked with surprise at the words ringing in my head, clear as a bell. Kalli's officious tone was unmistakable.

Yes, I know you hear me. Believe me, it's only the beginning of this part of our journey together. But, I'll shut up now and let you dispose of that body of mine. God, I'm glad to be rid of it! Awful old thing. Talk about cramping my style. Geesh!

And the voice was gone. I looked over to see Marc wrapping Kalli's body in a blanket. A few weeks before, we'd decided to cremate her body and not take possession of the ashes. Kay would handle these arrangements for us.

He looked up at me. "What?"

I shook my head. I'd tell him about Kalli's latest trick some other time.

With a heavy sigh, Marc cradled Kalli's body in his arms and followed Kay to her car. I trailed behind.

Kay's cattle dog, Liam, jerked to attention when we approached. He left his perch in the back seat as Kay opened the car door.

With a gentleness that brought a new wave of tears to my eyes, Marc settled the wrapped body onto the bench seat and stepped away. My eyes were pinned to the blanket bundle in Kay's car. The finality of it took my breath away.

Kay closed the door firmly and turned to face us. "That dog had an amazing life with you two. And you with her. Celebrate the memory of every minute of joy she brought you. And forget about this." Kay jerked her head toward the car. "It's not the important part."

After giving each of us tight hugs, Kay drove away.

Marc and I wandered into the house like zombies. The quiet of the place seared into my chest. My stomach roiled, as if someone had kicked me in the gut. Hard. I dropped onto the couch and stared at the last spot where Kalli had been.

Adrenaline hit in a rush. I jumped to my feet, drawing a surprised look from Marc as he sprawled in his chair. I had to move, to do something, to fill the space left barren and empty in Kalli's wake.

I snatched the incontinence pads from the floor and stalked into the laundry room. I threw the washed pads in the dryer and loaded the washer with the latest—and last—load. Cranking up the machine, I threw in detergent and slammed shut the lid.

As soon as I left the room, the phone rang.

"What are you doing?" Anita's voice came through the receiver, vigorous and calm.

"She's gone, Anita."

"I know, honey. Now, what are you doing?"

I sighed. "Cleaning up."

"Why?"

"Why not?"

"Because you're starting to wallow. Kalli isn't pleased about this."

No kidding, I'm not. Remember what Kay told you? Celebrate! Celebrate the wonderfulness that is me. For pity's sake, Mom, just because my body isn't around anymore—and let me say one more time, thank God—doesn't mean I'm not around. You're going to get sick of me in your head, believe me. Now, go. Play. Remember all the great times we had together and toast me with a glass of wine. Or two.

I realized Anita had been quiet as I'd listened to Kalli's words in my head. Now, she said, "You get all that?"

For the millionth time, I questioned what I'd "heard." Had it been my imagination?

"You know better than that," Anita snapped. "If I can hear what you were just thinking, why in the hell can't you accept that you're hearing Kalli? And just for the record, I heard her, too. Don't dismiss her voice as something you've made up. Kalli was opinionated when she lived in her physical form. Trust me, she's going to be that way from the Other Side, too. And you're going to hear every bit of what she has to say, whether you want to or not."

I chuckled at that.

Whoa. I chuckled. Even in the midst of my loss.

Well, I should hope so. Don't think I won't kick your butt if you get too maudlin over my stupid body going away, Mom. You're a drama queen. We all know it.

Anita laughed. "Well, I guess she told you. Now then, I suggest you collect that lovely husband of yours and hit the road. Go up into the mountains, find a pub with a great deck, and toast to Kalli's life."

"Yes, ma'am!"

I couldn't believe how much lighter I felt as I walked into the family room and told Marc what had just happened. He was skeptical that I was "hearing" Kalli in my head, but more than happy to get out of the house for a drink.

We spent the afternoon exactly as Anita and Kalli had prescribed—in the mountains, on the deck of a pub with an amazing vista spreading before us, splitting a bottle of wine.

LIFE CHANGES

Life without the physical Kalli was beyond difficult. Each stretch of highway around our house brought with it some memory of our spaniel. After all, Kalli and I had spent nearly every day for the nine years we'd lived in Colorado trooping down one trail or another.

The interior of the house and our yard were crammed with even more intense recollections of our beloved dog.

Grief wove its way into my heart in surprising ways and at unexpected times. Immersed in an activity, I'd suddenly find myself crying. A curve on the road would bring a view loaded with Kalli images. The tears would follow.

The most poignant moments arrived when I'd walk into the house after having been out for a time. The unnatural stillness of the rooms always rammed into my stomach. I couldn't turn on the television fast enough, even though its mindless chatter didn't ease the pain.

It was only time that soothed me at all…and the officious sound of Kalli in my head.

You didn't really think I'd go away, did you? Not likely. I signed on with you for your entire life. I told Grandma Anita to make sure you understood that. I'm guessing she did, but you're so busy being sad, you've forgotten.

That's okay, for now. We have time. We have years ahead of us. So, get used to me. And try to get on with your life, okay?

You know what that means, don't you? Another dog. Yup! I know it's impossible to even think I could be replaced. And of course, I really can't be in the truest sense because I'm so unique. But you need another furry buddy in your life. Someone who will love you and process for you, and keep you company, and...well, you get the point.

Mind you, it will be a very different kind of relationship than the one we have. And that's exactly as it should be.

"Don't wait too long to get another dog," Anita warned me when I told her about my most recent mental conversation with Kalli. "If you don't take the initiative, Kalli will select one for you."

"Oh, boy." I could just see a baby Great Dane on our doorstep after Marc and I had decided to adopt a little lap dog.

Anita chuckled. "Yes, you're getting the point."

As it turned out, Kalli backed off from her plans to bring us a puppy because Marc's and my living situation changed. We'd always felt we'd bought too large a home in Colorado. Now, without Kalli's physical presence, the large rooms seemed especially empty and cold. It was time to downsize.

We signed a contract with a real estate agent and put our house on the market. Our days became chaotic as we were never sure when we needed to leave the house for a showing. Clearly, the environment wasn't right for a new dog. We tabled the notion of adopting a pet and focused on stabilizing our lives.

A year passed, and the "For Sale" sign perched along the road aged with the progression of seasons. Finally, the spring brought with it a young couple who walked into our house and fell in love.

It was 2011 and banks were loath to lend money for mortgages. But our prospective buyers—a family doctor and an aerospace engineer, each gainfully employed with excellent credit and boatloads of cash—survived the hassles from the lending institutions. The deal was done. By the beginning of June, we had settled into a lovely townhouse in Littleton...complete with beautiful, campus-like grounds.

We'd found the ultimate dog-friendly community. It was time to adopt a new member of the family.

I hit the Internet in an eerie echo of the obsessive research I'd conducted to find Kalli. However, this time I haunted animal rescue sites, ignoring private breeders. In retrospect, I knew Kalli would have had a great home, even without us in the mix. Her breeder, Pam, would have made certain of that. Our next dog needed to be a rescue...an animal whose survival depended upon being adopted by us.

Within minutes of finding the website, PetFinder.com, I was overwhelmed. So many dogs desperate for loving humans. Where would I start? When I read the description of a Yorkie that said: "I'm just a little guy. I promise I won't take up too much room or get in your way..." I shut down the browser and reached for a tissue to wipe my tears.

Really, Mom? Some staffer wrote that to get your attention. And it worked. Look at your reaction! That Yorkie's a nasty little thing you wouldn't want within miles of you. Or more to the point, I don't want it within miles of you.

Geesh. Get a grip. If you're going to look for a dog with that sentimental attitude, you'll be a wreck before you even start.

Calm down. Think about all the things you want in your next dog. And listen to me. I'm here to help and guide you.

Weeks passed. Every listing that looked promising became a dead end. In the back of my mind, I knew Kalli was manipulating the situation, biding her time as she waited for just the right dog to come along. This was never clearer than the "circuit busy" buzzing across my phone line as I tried to call the Denver Dumb Friends League about an adoptable soft-coated wheaten terrier. It was only when I gave up and decided to move on to other listings that the phone functioned properly again.

Whew! That was a close one.

"Kalli, what the hell?" I groused.

You would have hated that dog...nothing but a stupid floor mop thing. Trust me.

"But to knock out the phone?"

I could almost see her shrug.

What can I say? You weren't paying attention to me.

Hard to believe.

Another instance, most likely manipulated by Kalli, involved a pair of Pekingese. The litter mates sounded adorable from their descriptions. The rescue organization wanted to adopt them together, and that was just fine with Marc and me. We'd take them both.

I grabbed Marc and we hit the road after calling to confirm they were still at the shelter...only to discover that minutes before we arrived, they'd been loaded into a van and transported to a sister facility in Colorado Springs. For just a moment, Marc and I flirted with the notion of following them downstate.

"Nope. Those two dogs weren't meant for us, clearly," Marc declared.

I could hear Kalli's sigh of relief.

That night, as I found myself compulsively plowing through rescue websites, I decided to take a break from finding our next dog. My emotions had grown a tad too intense for my liking.

Two weeks passed, during which time I avoided all websites having to do with dogs. And then on a whim, one Saturday morning, I decided to give PetFinders.com a quick look before Marc and I left for lunch. I wanted to avoid a broad search that would inundate me with listings. After all, I didn't have much time before we headed for the restaurant. I opted to limit my search to the bichon frisé. I chose this breed for no other reason than the memory of a bichon I'd met who had come the closest to rivaling Kalli's brilliance.

Relatively few animals popped up in the search, and I breezed through the listings. Until I saw the picture of a fuzzy ball of a dog. His back faced the camera as he hunched in the corner of a concrete cell. He peered at the lens over one shoulder, his eyes shy and hesitant under a fringe of thick eyelashes.

His name was Petey.

Freezing, I stared at the picture for long moments.

"What's wrong, Laura? You look like you've seen a ghost." Marc's voice sounded faint as I scanned the dog's description:

"Petey is an all-round good dog. He was found as a stray, but the finders kept him long enough to know he's housetrained and good with people of all ages, and both dogs and cats. He's good on leash. Petey has a great personality!"

I was hooked. I looked up and met Marc's eyes.

"Let's go," I said in quiet tones. "I've found our dog."

As I pushed my laptop across the coffee table so Marc could see Petey, the phone rang. Anita wanted to talk to Marc. She had a computer problem.

A sudden sense of urgency hit me as Marc began to answer Anita's questions.

"Call her back on your cell from the car," I whispered, trying to calm myself.

Marc absentmindedly nodded and continued talking.

Geesh, Mom. Get him out the door. You guys have to go now!

Ah, yes, the source of my inner pressure was Kalli. What a surprise.

"Marc," I hissed, pointing at Petey's picture on the computer screen.

"Uh, Anita. Laura and I were just heading out," Marc told our friend. "Could I call you right back from the car?"

And we were on our way.

Petey resided in a shelter in Pueblo, Colorado…about an hour's drive from our townhouse. We steered the car south on I-25 and sped down the interstate.

The woman at the shelter's reception desk stared at us with bored eyes until we told her we wanted to see Petey. Her face lit up. "Oh, that's great. You're going to love him. He's one of our favorites." She spoke into a phone, then turned back to us. "Angie will be right down to take you back there."

I tried to ignore the sea of dogs on all sides of me as we followed Angie down the hallway, but the frantic barks and desperate eyes were tough to overlook. When Angie finally stopped in front of one of the

kennels, I peered through the glass. I didn't see a fuzzy, little white dog matching Petey's picture, but I did see a close-clipped guy whose eyes I recognized.

"Yup, that's him. He just got back from the groomer's," Angie said as she entered his cell. Petey looked me in the eyes as I stopped in front of him. He leaned against one concrete wall, appearing to shrink away from his cellmates—a pair of miniature schnauzers whose frenzied barking had reached a fevered pitch with Angie's presence. I imagined I saw Petey sigh as he glanced at them, then returned his steady gaze to me.

Angie ignored the schnauzers as she hooked a leash onto Petey's collar and guided him from the concrete room. She handed the leash to me and off we went to a small yard behind the shelter. Petey walked by our sides confidently, easily. As if he'd been with us for years.

I looked at Marc, and he smiled back at me.

"He's clearly not a bichon," I said softly.

"But you're in love, anyway." Marc's smile widened.

I turned back to Angie. "He's perfect. We'll take him."

An impromptu farewell committee hovered by the exit as we finished filling out the paperwork. I looked into the faces of the staff and volunteers as they threw their arms around Petey, telling him how much they loved him and wishing us well.

The little guy trotted past his fan club, acknowledging them with careful politeness. His manners demanded he respond to them, but his survival instincts honed in on us with the accuracy of a laser beam.

He's been through a lot and he's been hurt, Mom. Be sensitive to that, sure, but don't feel too sorry for him. That's the worst thing you can do with a rescue dog...that pity thing. Trust me. He's very bright, and he's fully capable of using your emotions to manipulate you. Then, you'll have a little monster on your hands. And that would be unacceptable.

Remember all the stuff you learned when you thought you were training me? Be a little softer with him than you were with me, but stick to the same principles Kristen showed you. And be patient with him because you're no long dealing with the wonderfulness of the secure dog I was.

He's a sweet kid and has good stuff in him. He's willing and able to work with you and for you. Frankly, he's perfect for you and Daddy.

Great job, Mommy. You listened to me as I picked just the right dog for you. Of course we've always known how good I am at everything. But I've really outdone myself this time, haven't I?

PETEY

With Kalli's stamp of approval, Petey moved into our hearts and home with the gratitude and loyalty that can only come from a dog who knows he's been rescued. The joy shared among the three of us became even sweeter as we reflected on Petey's story. Piecing together what the shelter knew and Anita "heard" about him, our hearts ached for him.

His first home had been loving. For some reason—Anita couldn't pick up the specifics—he moved into a second place as a favor to his original owner, who could no longer keep him. Petey's new humans didn't want him, abused him, and dumped him on the streets. A family found him, brought him into their home, and mounted a serious search for his owners. When no one stepped up to claim him, they took him to the shelter where he'd resided for a few weeks before we entered his life.

It didn't take long for us to learn Petey was haunted by this difficult past. Nasty hints raised their ugly heads at odd moments. One day when I brought out the broom, Petey dropped to the floor and slunk upstairs to hide under our bed for hours. Similarly shaped objects elicited the same reaction.

The first time I swore in annoyance—I'd cut myself chopping vegetables—terrorized him. In fact, the slightest show of irritation by his humans—even when it wasn't directed at him—paralyzed him with fear.

His first few car trips were filled with anxious whimpering. When he realized he was returning to his home with us, he calmed immediately.

I refused to contemplate why his lower jaw was distinctly out of alignment with the upper jaw. Instead, I focused on the resultant and adorable underbite. But my campaign to curb an overactive imagination that taunted me with visions of what his life must have been like before we adopted him was only partially successful.

From Anita's insight and a quick vet checkup, we discovered that he was in good health, and guessed he was older than two years of age and younger than four. Given the relatively blank slate of his past, we couldn't be more specific. We were able to determine his breed, however. A DNA test showed him to be a "schnug," which is a recognized "designer" mix of miniature schnauzer and pug.

Weighing in at twenty-three pounds, he expressed himself through his beautiful brown pug eyes. His fur shone with the fawn color of his pug parent, and was the texture and length of a schnauzer. He sported pug ears. The curly pug tail was fluffy with schnauzer fur, and beneath an elongated pug body were the graceful legs of his schnauzer parent. The mix of the two breeds was unmistakable once you knew what it was.

"You know, if his breed hadn't been misidentified, you never would have found him," Marc said, smiling at me from his armchair one afternoon. It was a few months after we'd adopted Petey and I had just remarked, yet again, how weird it was that the shelter staff had thought Petey was a bichon. He went on, "This has Kalli's touch all over it—the coincidence of their mistake and the way you defined such a breed-specific search that morning. You'd never done that before. Why it occurred to you then…"

"I couldn't agree more." As I studied Petey from across the room, he lifted his head to look at me. Suddenly, his eyebrows raised, just like Kalli's used to.

"Um, Marc? Have you ever noticed Petey raising his eyebrows?"

"You mean like that look Kalli would give us? No, can't say I have. I loved it when Kalli did that, didn't you?"

"Uh huh. And I saw him do it. Just now."

Marc stared at me, then started laughing. "You don't suppose…"

"Kalli's coaching him? Wouldn't put it past her."

I suppose our imaginations were getting the better of us, to think Kalli had encouraged Petey's behavior. Then again, the notion wasn't beyond the realm of possibility and occurred to me every time I got the Kalli-like "look" from Petey from that moment on.

As long as we established careful boundaries around Petey, life for our resident canine was relatively calm. That meant we had to find a mobile groomer and vet who'd come to us. The notion of taking Petey out of his home to put him in a cage at a commercial establishment around other crated dogs seemed abhorrent given his painful past and time at the shelter. I didn't want to ask more from him than my instincts told me he was capable of giving easily.

Petey seemed to rejoice in his dogly status in our household, although there were times when he carried his dogginess a bit too far. While someone had taken the time to train him in the basics, and his manners were impeccable with other humans and dogs, wastebasket contents were a bit too enticing to him for our liking.

When we left him at home, we made certain those wastebaskets—and food stuffs—were off-limits for his protection and the sake of our nerves. One incident in which he raided our pantry through an unlatched door was enough. I'm grateful he survived eating that half-pound of brown sugar. We had no intention of pushing our luck in the future.

Anita got a major kick out of him, often marveling over how different he was from his predecessor. Once when I asked her how he responded to an encounter we had on a walk the day before, she laughed for long moments.

"Honey," she finally gasped, "that dog has long forgotten what happened yesterday. Seriously, you could ask Kalli that kind of question and get a cogent answer, but this dog is as different from her as night and day."

She added in a quiet voice, "If he had Kalli's analytical ability and memory, Petey never would have made it. He would have died years ago. But as it is, he's the ultimate survivor because he focuses on the here and now. And that's all he needs for a happy life with you."

That insight made life with Petey all the more special. He was secure and loved…surrounded by the same support network that had stabilized Kalli's life. Kay visited monthly, Dina checked in regarding his training, and Anita carried on conversations with him, albeit in a limited fashion. The future was bright for our little rescue, thanks in no small part to Kalli.

I have no doubt Kalli guided him to us. And what better way to end a book about her life than to celebrate her legacy through Petey? Of course, her involvement with me continues in a more direct fashion. Indeed, her words resonate in my head regularly.

Hummph! It's about time you finished this book about me. Geesh, what took you so long, for pity's sake?

Each time I hear her, I realize she will always be with me. And I reflect on how much more than a dog she remains in my life.

ABOUT THE PHOTOGRAPHER

Photographer/writer **David Sutton** has a keen eye for capturing the shared humanity between people and their animals.

Since 1994 Sutton has specialized in an artful approach to pet-centric family portraiture. He brings a warm, insightful and whimsical style to his portraits, with a strong emphasis on relationships.

David's distinctive black-and-white work has earned him accolades over twenty years, including the unique honor of being named the best pet photographer in America by the magazine *Forbes FYI*. Sutton Studios' charitable work has helped to raise over a million dollars for more than a hundred animal and human welfare agencies.

ABOUT THE ILLUSTRATOR

Rian Miller is a cartoonist and artist living in Alpharetta, Georgia. She has been drawing since she was a child and has also taken interest in all kinds of cartoons. Her designs and cartoons have appeared on various blogs and websites and other multi-media projects. Her other interests include anime, music, movies, webcomics, costuming, and animation. Visit her art at jaspersart.blogspot.com

ABOUT THE AUTHOR

Laura Abbott is a professional writer who shares her love of dogs with her husband, Marc. The couple lives with Kalli's successor—Petey, the schnauzer/pug rescue—at the base of the Rocky Mountain foothills in Littleton, Colorado.

You can visit Laura at her website:
www.LauraAbbottBooks.com.

Made in the USA
Columbia, SC
02 February 2020